W9-BNT-842

FRANCISCAN PRAYER

Franciscan Prayer

ILIA DELIO, O.S.F.

ST. ANTHONY MESSENGER PRESS

Cincinnati, Ohio

Nihil Obstat: Rev. David L. Zink
   Hilarion Kistner, O.F.M.
Imprimi Potest: Fred Link, O.F.M.
Imprimatur: Most Rev. Carl K. Moeddel
   Vicar General and Auxiliary Bishop of the Archdiocese of Cincinnati
   June 7, 2004

The *nihil obstat* and *imprimatur* are a declaration that a book or pamphlet is considered to be free from doctrinal or moral error. It is not implied that those who have granted the *nihil obstat* and *imprimatur* agree with the contents, opinions or statements expressed.

For Sister Lisa Marie Drover, C.S.S.F
Whose friendship has taught me
about prayer and God

Contents

Acknowledgments

Every book reflects a human journey. It is written for oneself and others, that each person who reads the work may see something of their own life in it—a reflection of their own journey. My Franciscan prayer class at the Washington Theological Union inspired this book. Gathering each week to discuss the principles and implications of prayer in the Franciscan tradition, I began to see how the deepening of prayer in the human heart reflects the face of God in the believer. It is with them in mind that I wrote this book. I would like to thank several people, however, who contributed to the fine-tuning of the work. I am grateful to Dr. Timothy Johnson for his careful reading of the text and helpful suggestions, Steven Kluge, O.F.M., for his comments and commendations, Cyprian Rosen, O.F.M., CAP., for reading the work and helpful discussion, Dr. Thelma Steiger whose insights on the imitation of Christ were influential in shaping the chapter on this subject and Cynthia Rogers for her gracious assistance. May all who drink from the fountain of Franciscan prayer never thirst for life. For Christ is the source of life and those who are in Christ are called to be life for the world.

Introduction

One day I was sitting in the dining room at the Washington Theological Union where I teach engaging a group of new students in conversation. A young woman turned to me and asked, "What are you teaching this semester?" I enthusiastically replied, "A course on Franciscan prayer." "Franciscan prayer," she exclaimed, "what is that? I know that the Carmelites have a tradition of prayer—but the Franciscans?" Although I had already prepared the course for the semester, the young woman's question took me by surprise. I was about to teach a course on a tradition of prayer that seemed highly dubious. I had done my homework for the course, but the question continued to linger with me throughout the semester and in subsequent years as I began to ponder more deeply the question, what is Franciscan prayer?

I must admit that my own spiritual journey began in a cloister of discalced Carmelite nuns where I spent four years learning the art of monastic prayer. When I eventually found my way into Franciscan life, it was my Carmelite foundation of prayer that provided the framework for my relationship with God. It was not long before I discovered that Franciscan life is different from Carmelite life, not only in the structure of the life itself but in the way the life forms one's spiritual attitudes of relationship to God, to others and to the world. Both forms of life add their beauty to the mystical Body of Christ, but Franciscan life is not monastic, and my Carmelite-shaped path of prayer needed to find a new voice and a new spirit in the cloister of the world.

So this is a book on Franciscan prayer written by a theologian who strives to define more clearly the path of Franciscan prayer and as one who seeks God in a complex world. It is my belief that an understanding of prayer in the Franciscan tradition, that is, the spirituality of prayer, can offer new vitality to Christian life today because it is a path of relationship with God that strives to live in the fullness of the Incarnation. It is a path that can enkindle the fire of Christian life by lifting us out of the doldrums of mediocrity and complacency and draw us into the mystery of Christ.

Franciscan prayer is dynamic because it is about participation in the mystical Body of Christ. Prayer in this tradition is decisively incarnational; it is centered on the person of Jesus Christ. According to Franciscan theology, Christ cannot be separated from the Trinity because Jesus Christ is the Word of God incarnate, the One through whom all things are made and in whom all things find their completion. To enter into the mystery of Christ through prayer, therefore, is to enter into the mystery of the Trinity, and to live in the Trinity is to live in relationships of love. Because Franciscan prayer is focused on the person of Christ, it is affective. It is prayer of the heart rather than head, and it seeks to center one's heart in God. The heart that is centered in God views the world as the place where God dwells.

Franciscan prayer is contemplative and cosmic. It is a type of prayer that impels one to find God in the vast corners of the universe. Because of the Incarnation, the Word made flesh, all of creation is holy; all of creation is the sacrament of God. Prayer is that relationship with God which opens the eyes of believers to the sanctity of all life—from earthworms to humans, from quarks to stars. Everything that exists reflects the goodness of God. Prayer is the breath of the Holy Spirit within us that opens our eyes to the divine good which saturates our world.

Finally, Franciscan prayer is evangelizing. It is an awakening to the Good News of Jesus Christ and to the love of God poured out for us in Christ. Those who seek God along the path of Franciscan prayer are to be transformed by the one they seek, the one they claim to love. Prayer centered on relationship with Christ, the Word of God incarnate, cannot help but change the life of the believer and the way one lives.

Those who enter into Franciscan prayer, therefore, must be ready for change; they each must be willing to become "another Christ," for this is where the path of prayer leads, to a new birth of Christ in the lives of the believers. The Russian Orthodox liken prayer to entering the cave of a tiger—the experience is uncontrollable. Risk is involved and yet, too, a certain level of trust. Prayer that leads to real participation in the mystery of Christ, or we might say, prayer that allows the mystery of Christ to change our lives, is a high-risk enterprise—an uncontrollable experience. Yet, the power of God's grace is such that one who, like Francis of Assisi, is able to trust God sufficiently can enter into the "cave" of the heart, the place where Incarnation takes place, and be transformed into the triumph of love. Franciscan prayer, therefore, is Christ-centered, affective, contemplative, cosmic and evangelizing. The goal of prayer is to make Jesus Christ alive in the believer. To bring Christ to life is the way to peace.

To understand the significance of Franciscan prayer is to identify some of the major voices of the tradition and the way they have described this particular path of relationship with God. I have chosen to bring into dialogue three major voices—Francis of Assisi, Clare of Assisi and Bonaventure of Bagnoregio—who form a trinity of complementary thoughts that help define the Franciscan way to God. There are other voices in the tradition who have spoken on prayer, for example, Angela of Foligno and Ramón Lull, but these three voices form a foundation of prayer that characterizes the tradition. While Francis of Assisi inspired a gospel way of life that came to be known as "Franciscan," Clare of Assisi was a cornerstone of this foundation and contributed a feminine voice to the development of the Franciscan movement. Bonaventure was a trained theologian and Minister General of the Order who combined the spirituality of Francis with the Christian theological tradition to form a Franciscan theological worldview.

Both Francis and Clare lived in the thirteenth century in the town of Assisi. Francis was born around 1181 and died in 1226; Clare was born in 1193 and died in 1253. Although Clare was twelve years younger than Francis, her life was no less ambitious in the pursuit of holiness than that of Francis. There are many modern biographies that recount the life of Francis; however, the details remain obscure because of the historical circumstances in which he lived. His rapid rise to official sanctity (he was canonized two years after his death) has made it difficult to extract the person of Francis from the saint, Francis, although modern scholarship has made tremendous strides in this respect.

In the Middle Ages there were several noteworthy biographers of Francis' life. Brother Thomas of Celano (d. 1260) was "the first to write a life of Saint Francis and the first to describe the earliest days of the life of his followers."[1] Drawing from the memory of the martyrs, the ascetics and the monks, Thomas showed that Francis is a saint rooted in the tradition of the church.[2] His *Life of Saint Francis* is divided into three books. The theme of "the humility of the Incarnation" identifies Book One. In Book Two, the "charity of the Passion" predominates; and Book Three, which recounts the canonization and miracles, describes the liturgy of Francis that continues to be celebrated on earth. It bears witness to the renewed Spirit of healing and life which Francis' life imparted to the community left behind.[3] The official biography of the Franciscan Order was written around 1260 by Bonaventure, who was Minister General of the Order for seventeen years.[4] Bonaventure wrote two works, *The Major Legend of Saint Francis* and a shorter work, *The Minor Legend of Saint Francis*, devised for liturgical use. The term *legenda* indicates that these works were intended for public reading by the brothers and the wider Christian community.[5] Bonaventure was requested by the Franciscan Order at the Chapter of Narbonne in 1260 to write the *Major Legend* so that the Order would have a standardized biography of Francis, more aptly, one good legend from all the existing ones. He relied on the texts of Thomas of Celano and another biographer, Julian of Speyer, to construct his biography, which has a distinct Christocentric lens through which he interprets the life of Francis. Bonaventure's work became the fundamental, primary portrait of Francis and, next to Francis' *Rule* and *Testament*, the principal interpreter of his vision.[6]

It is surprising that a small, carefree cloth merchant from a little medieval town in Umbria could ignite a spiritual revolution. But indeed, Francis of Assisi seems to have done just that. Starting out as a rather self-centered young man who enjoyed the social life, Francis was somewhat of a rogue and a dreamer who lived in the age of chivalry and courtly love. He longed to become a valiant knight and taste the glory of victory. However, after being wounded in battle early in his military career his dreams were somewhat shattered. Finding himself in what today we might call a "soldier's hospital," he began to consider his life more deeply. During this period Francis had a profound experience of God that had a significant influence on the direction of his life. After regaining his health he did not return to battle, rather he began to wander into abandoned churches and lonely places to pray. Eventually he renounced his worldly life and committed himself to a gospel or evangelical way of life.

Francis did not invent evangelical life, although his popularity certainly helped the rise of this movement among lay Christians in the Middle Ages. Rather, in the late twelfth and thirteenth centuries there was a great desire to follow Jesus Christ without entering a monastery. Men such as Peter Waldo, a married businessperson, renounced their families and possessions and took up a life of begging for alms and preaching the gospel.[7] Women known as "Beguines" embarked on a committed gospel way of life in their own homes, following a regimen of fasting, prayer and penance.[8] The conversion of Francis around 1205/1206 and the decision to live a radical gospel way of life took place within the spirit of the thirteenth century and its enthusiasm for evangelical life. However, Francis was not a mere follower. As he tells us in his *Testament*, he felt that his way of life had been divinely inspired. "No one showed me what I had to do," he wrote, "but the Most High himself revealed to me that I should live according to the pattern of the holy gospel."[9] Because Francis' way of life was attractive to others it enjoyed rapid growth. To ensure his way of life, Francis had to write a *Rule* that provided guidelines to the life. Beginning with a small Rule based on the gospel (the *propositum vitae*), Francis eventually composed the *Earlier Rule* of 1221 that contained much of his own thought and spirituality. This Rule was later revised and shortened and became the *Later Rule* of 1223, the official Rule of the Franciscan Order.

Francis begins his Rule by stating that "the Rule and Life...is to observe the Holy Gospel of Our Lord Jesus Christ,"[10] indicating that his way of life is based on the person of Jesus Christ, that is, the Good News of God dwelling among us. Francis' way of evangelical life is defined by how one experiences the presence of God through Christ.[11] This experience of God in the flesh should orient the follower of Christ to being a "person in relationship," that is, a sister or brother. Community marks the life of Francis. Through his following of Christ, Francis became a brother first to the poor and sick, and ultimately to all of creation.

Thomas of Celano provides three basic intuitions of Francis that inspired his path of evangelical life. First, he indicates that Francis perceived that the world is good and provides for authentic human needs. While the world is filled with God's overflowing goodness, it is poverty that allows one to experience this goodness by becoming radically dependent on God. Second, for Francis the meaning of creation and thus of the human person is revealed and manifest in Jesus Christ. It is in and through Christ that Francis discovers the meaning of his own life, the dignity of the human person, and the goodness of creation. Finally, Francis' vision of the crucified seraph and the Stigmata (the wounds of Christ) reveal to him that the human person, like Christ, is fragile, limited and vulnerable.[12] Francis himself grew in compassionate love, like Christ, willing to give his life for the sake of the other. These three aspects of Francis' "evangelical world view" (creation, Incarnation, human person) all point to the fact that, for Francis, the human person is the fundamental category of experience. It is the person of Jesus Christ who reveals to him the dignity of all persons and that of creation itself.[13] For Francis, the only "work" that is fundamental to his way of life is to imitate Christ and to make that experience of Christ available to others.[14] Evangelical life focuses on what we are, not what we do. The goal of the life is to be a sister or brother to all, announcing the Good News in one's example and deeds. Using the language of Clare, it is to become a mirror (of Christ) and footprint (of Christ) for others to see and follow. The goal of the life is participation in the body of Christ united in the Spirit of love.

Francis had his own perception of God and God's relation to the world through Jesus Christ. His "theological intuitions" were original and became the basis of "Franciscan theology." Recently, scholars have referred to Francis as a "vernacular theologian" because he described a God-world relationship based on his own experience and described it in his own language of spirituality.[15] One of the great theologians of the Franciscan Order was Bonaventure of Bagnoregio (1217–1274) who, as we indicated, was also the seventh Minister General of the Order. Bonaventure had the unique gift of synthesis and brought together the theological insights of Francis, such as the goodness of God and the centrality of Christ, with the classical works of Augustine, Bernard of Clairvaux and other writers of the tradition. In this way Bonaventure created a theological "worldview," that is, a vision of the interconnectedness between God, humanity and creation that was distinctly Franciscan.[16] His spiritual writings emphasized love and union with Christ crucified as the path to God. It was Bonaventure who saw Francis as the man of peace and who wrote that prayer is the way to peace.[17] In Bonaventure's view, to be a person of prayer one had to be a person of desire. And to be a person of desire, one had to be willing to travel the path of the burning love of the crucified Christ.

Bonaventure's theology of prayer, with its focus on contemplation and the centrality of Christ crucified, complements Francis' own writings on prayer, which is at the heart of his life. In his *Later Rule* Francis wrote, "Desire above all things (*supra omnia*) to have the Spirit of the Lord and its holy activity, [and] to pray always with a pure heart."[18] The idea that prayer is essential to Franciscan life, however, has not always been emphasized. (What? Franciscans have a tradition of prayer?) Francis' ministry to the lepers and his preaching the gospel seem to have overshadowed the centrality of prayer in his way of life. Further, while Francis held up prayer as the basis for following Christ, his writings on prayer are scattered throughout his letters, rules and dictated writings. The biographers of Francis tell us that he prayed, that he prayed unceasingly and that he came to resemble Christ through a prayerful loving relationship with Christ. However, we do not know *how* prayer led him to become "another Christ" and a man of peace. Francis himself did not provide any real "road-map" or *Itinerarium* of prayer for evangelical life. Bonaventure certainly attempted to outline

Francis' path to peace in his *Soul's Journey into God,* but the difficulty of this work with its complex, symbolic theology did not prove to be accessible to a wider audience. So we have the centrality of the gospel in Francis' way of life and the centrality of prayer, but until now it has been unclear how these two central focal points are integrally related. Until we come to Clare of Assisi.

Scholars tell us that Clare desired to follow Francis' evangelical way of life and may indeed have done so in the early part of her career. At the age of eighteen, she left her noble household in upper Assisi to join Francis and the brothers at the little church of the Portiuncula ("Our Lady of the Angels") in the Umbrian valley below the town of Assisi. What is unclear is how long she and her companions stayed with the brothers. Because it was considered unsafe for women in the Middle Ages to live independently or without some type of male protection, we are told that Francis placed Clare and her sisters in a Benedictine monastery, eventually moving them to the convent of San Damiano where Clare remained until her death. Although she described herself as *"la piantacella,"*[19] the little plant of Francis, she was clearly no wilting flower. She had a strong, independent spirit and a real desire to join in Francis' evangelical project. Whereas Francis saw poverty as the means for living authentic gospel life, Clare fought for the "privilege of poverty," because poverty was the key to Christian life. The Incarnation spoke to her of the "poverty of God" manifested in God's self-giving love. Her fight for this privilege was compounded by the fact that she lived under the Benedictine Rule throughout most of her life.[20] Although the tools of historical-critical analysis are now helping to retrieve a more authentic Clare, it is apparent that she never succumbed to the monastic spirit. Rather, she continued to fight for the "privilege of poverty," which she won about a year before her death in 1253.[21] She wrote her own Rule and was the first woman of the church to have a Rule officially approved for a community of women.

What makes Clare an important figure in a book on Franciscan prayer is that she provides the "roadmap" of prayer for evangelical life. I believe she was able to do this precisely because she lived under a monastic rule while ardently desiring evangelical life. In other words, to really cling to what she believed in, she had to consolidate its meaning for herself and those who followed her. As we will see in Chapter Three, the monastic path to God is quite different from the evangelical path. It emphasizes divine transcendence rather than immanence, the ascended Christ rather than the crucified Christ, spiritual union with God rather than the physical expression of divine love. The monastic quest includes the silence and solitude of the cloister to seek God whereas evangelical life, with its focus on the Incarnation, means that God is to be found in the cloister of the world. As far as we know, Clare wrote only four short letters to the noblewoman of Bohemia, Agnes of Prague, whom she never met but with whom she shared a spiritual bond, describing Agnes as "half of her soul."[22] Although Clare also wrote a Rule and Testament,[23] it is her letters, rich and dense in spirituality, which reflect her evangelical spirit. In her second letter to Agnes she lays out the path to union with God centered on the mystery of Christ crucified. Because this passage provides the structure of this book, I quote it here:

> O most noble Queen, gaze [on him], consider [him], contemplate [him], as you desire to imitate [him]. If you suffer with him, you will reign with him. [If you] weep [with him], you shall rejoice with him; [if you] die with him on the cross of tribulation, you shall possess heavenly mansions in the splendor of the saints and, in the Book of Life, your name shall be called glorious among people.[24]

Gaze—consider—contemplate—imitate. What makes this passage significant is the way it parallels the monastic ascent to God and yet clearly differs from it. The monastic ascent begins with the reading of Scripture which leads to meditation, then prayer and contemplation. Clare begins with a "visual reading," a gazing on the image of the crucified Christ, which leads to meditation or consideration of Christ, then to contemplation and imitation of Christ. Whereas the monastic path ends at contemplation, for Clare, the goal of prayer is imitation. It is not simply that we arrive at union with God; rather, it is that we become what we love. Prayer is to forge us into the likeness of the beloved, and thus it is bringing Christ to life in the believer. This is evangelical life—bringing Christ to life by participating in the Christ mystery. Prayer is the energy of evangelical life because it transforms the desire for gospel life into the practice of gospel living. Clare's template of prayer, gaze—consider—contemplate—imitate, is the template of evangelical life and the relationship with God that makes this life alive. Because this template complements the spirituality of Francis and Bonaventure, I have used it to construct a path of prayer for Franciscan evangelical life.

In order to explore this path of prayer, I begin with the basis of prayer, the divine-human relationship and the desire for God, which form the first two chapters. Prayer is that relationship with God, the longing of the human heart for God, and God's longing for us. Franciscan prayer is about relationship with a God of overflowing love. It is discovering the God of love at the center of our lives and of our world and finding the truth of our identity in God. To enter into this relationship one must be a person of desire. God does not force us into a relationship of love but freely gives us the grace to respond to his invitation of love. Spiritual desire is the longing of the heart for relationship with God that brings happiness and peace. Francis of Assisi was a passionate person, a dreamer, a lover and a person of desire. When he felt his desire filled in hearing the gospel, he found the answer to his deepest longings and changed his life accordingly. He became a follower of Christ. Francis' life shows us that we must be attentive to our desires if we are to find the fulfillment of our lives in God.

Since prayer is the desire for God who is the source of our lives, it is the life-giving spirit that directs our life's journey. The third chapter explores the journey to God according to the path of Franciscan evangelical prayer. In order to highlight the Franciscan path, I discuss the monastic ascent to God in the context of Neoplatonism, which is a hierarchical view of God and world that gives priority to spiritual nature over material nature. Clare's fourfold path of prayer is then introduced as the path of Franciscan prayer. This path begins with encountering a God of compassionate love in the cross of Jesus Christ and ends in becoming the compassionate love of Christ in one's own life. Because poverty makes room for love and the indwelling of the Spirit, it is poverty that allows one to see or gaze on the mystery of God who comes to us in fragile humanity. Chapter Four examines the meaning of poverty for the Franciscans and the way poverty opens the path to prayer or relationship with God. As one enters more closely into relationship with God by entering more deeply into relationship with Christ, one becomes a friend of Christ. Just as in human friendship there is a spirit of solidarity, rejoicing together in good times and comforting one another in times of sorrow, so too the one who becomes a friend of Christ through prayer begins to experience solidarity with Christ. Chapter Five looks at friendship with Christ and how Francis, Clare and Bonaventure view friendship in light of the crucified Christ.

Prayer that leads to friendship requires a heart turned toward God. The human heart is the center of the human person, that center which directs our lives. "...where your treasure is, there your heart will also be," Jesus said (Luke 12:34). A wounded broken heart can lie in many fragmented pieces, scattered in many places. Broken hearts (which can live under the guise of smiling faces) are seeds for a broken world. And the longer a heart is broken, the more difficult it is to heal its wounds. Violence is often the result of broken hearts. Prayer that begins with the desire for wholeness and with a cry for God's mercy is that grace or life of the Spirit within us that binds up the wounds of the heart and turns it toward God. The Franciscan path of prayer, which leads one into the mystery of Christ, requires that the heart be centered in God. Chapter Six, therefore, looks at the centrality of the heart, especially in the writings of Francis and Bonaventure, and examines how we can turn our hearts to God in order to seek our happiness and peace.

According to Bonaventure, the heart centered in God is the heart that can see into the depths of things. Franciscan prayer is contemplative because it nurtures a relationship with Christ, the Word of God, in such a way that one comes to see the hidden presence of God in ordinary reality. Contemplation is a penetrating gaze with the eyes of the heart that sees the truth of things or, we might say, that sees the overflowing goodness of God in concrete reality. For the Franciscans, there is no such thing as "brute matter." Everything that exists, every person, plant and creature, everything is created out of the infinite goodness of God and expresses that goodness by its own existence. Since God's love is incarnate in Christ, we may say that everything in some way expresses Christ because everything that exists is, in some way, an incarnation of God's love. In short, the entire creation is holy and a sacrament of God. Prayer that leads one into the mystery of Christ leads one to recognize the overflowing goodness of God at the heart of creation. Chapter Seven explores contemplation and how the Franciscan path of prayer leads one to this new vision of reality. Here, Clare's profound insight with regard to contemplation and self-identity is discussed in view of Christ crucified. Clare describes the path to God as an integral relation between contemplation and transformation through self-identity. One must come to know who one is before God, one's strengths and weaknesses, gifts and failings, in order that one may be transformed into a vessel of compassionate love and come to see the world with new and deeper vision.

The Franciscan path of prayer that leads to contemplative vision leads to a greater union in love. The thirteenth-century penitent and mystic, Angela of Foligno, said, "as we see, so we love and the more perfectly and purely we see, the more perfectly and purely we love."[25] Ultimately, we are to become what we love, and since prayer is to lead to the fullness of love in union with Christ, we are to become "another Christ." Francis of Assisi was so filled with compassionate love, Bonaventure claims, that at the end of his life he looked like Christ, especially as he bore the wounds of Christ in his flesh (the Stigmata). Imitation of Christ is the goal of a prayerful relationship with God. Chapter Eight explores the meaning of "imitation," and the imitation of Christ as full participation in the Christ mystery. Christian life, beginning with baptism, is "putting on" Christ so that Christ may live in the believer. Franciscan evangelical life strives to live in this mystery more deeply through a life of unceasing prayer. God is to descend and take on flesh anew in our lives through the indwelling Spirit that joins us to Christ and expresses itself in the body of the believer. Prayer is the breath of the Spirit within us, the Spirit who brought about the Incarnation of the Word of God and who continues to incarnate the Word in our lives. The one Spirit who joins together the Father and Word in love brings us finite creatures into this infinite relationship of love. Because the one Spirit is sent by the one Christ, the fullness of Christ is the fullness of love that is the work of Spirit. The Spirit not only forms one to Christ but brings all into unity in Christ. In short, the Christ mystery is incomplete without our participation. The prayer attributed to the Carmelite saint, Teresa of Avila, illuminates this mystery:

> Christ has no body now on earth but yours, no hands but
> yours, no feet but yours. Yours are the eyes through which
> must look out Christ's compassion on the world. Yours are
> the feet with which he is to go about doing good. Yours are
> the hands with which he is to bless people now.[26]

The idea that our lives are intertwined with the mystery of Christ is at the heart of Franciscan evangelical life. That we *are* the body of Christ and how our bodies become the body of Christ is the path of Franciscan prayer. It is prayer that brings Christ to life in the believer and leads us to a "mysticism of maternity," that is, giving birth to Christ in our lives and in the life of the world.

The life of Christ is the life of *all* life—the peace of creation, the justice of humanity and the unity of humankind. That is why the Franciscan path of prayer must ultimately lead to peace because it leads to the compassionate love of the crucified Christ. Peace is the fruit of love. Francis became a person of peace because he became a person of love—a love shown in his body and in his willingness to spend himself for others. Bonaventure claims the road to peace begins with the desire for God and travels through the burning love of the crucified Christ. There is no peace without love, and there is no real love without suffering. The final chapter examines the path to peace as the imitation of Christ and the willingness to love compassionately like Christ. It focuses on the centrality of the Eucharist in the life of Francis and the imitation of Christ as the bodily expression of love. The Franciscan path of prayer that leads to peace is a path of transformation and witness. Christ is proclaimed not by words but by the example of one's life, one's willingness to suffer or perhaps offer one's life for the sake of another. Christ lives in that Christ lives in us—in our bodies, our hands, our feet and our actions. This is the challenge for our time with its emphasis on rationality and materialism, the challenge of divine risk, of allowing God to enter our lives and lift us out of the doldrums of mediocrity, privatism and individualism. We are called to be vulnerable to grace so that we may be transformed into the living Christ.

Franciscan prayer, lived to its full, is to set the human heart on fire. It is to transform one's body into a body of love and one's actions into actions of love. In this transformation is the fire that can set the earth ablaze—the fire of light, peace, justice, unity and dignity. It is to see the wounds of suffering humanity and bind them with mercy and compassion. It is to see and feel for all creation—to love by way of self-gift. It is to live in the mystery of Christ, the mystery of God en-fleshed. The mystery of being human lies in the mystery of desire, which shapes our lives and can change us. Only prayer can transform us into what we desire, that is, if we truly desire God. Prayer is to make real the Word made flesh—in our lives and in our world. Prayer is the Spirit of the Word that transforms our flesh into the body of Christ. It is an awakening to who we are in Christ and to the fact that we are the path to peace. The Franciscan path of prayer leads one to proclaim by example and deed: Jesus Christ lives!

NOTES

[1] *Francis of Assisi: Early Documents,* volume 1, *The Saint,* edited by Regis J. Armstrong, J. A. Wayne Hellmann, and William J. Short (New York: New City Press, 1999), 171. This English edition of Francis' writings and the first life by Thomas of Celano will hereafter be referred to as *FA:ED* I followed by page number. The critical edition of Francis' writings is *François d'Assise: Écrits,* intro., trans., and notes, Theophile Desbonnets, Thaddée Matura, Jean-François Godet, Damien Vorreux, *Source Crétiennes,* number 285 (Paris: Les Editions du Cerf, 1981).

[2] "Introduction to The Life of Saint Francis by Thomas of Celano," in *FA:ED* I, 175.

[3] Ibid., in *FA:ED* I, 177.

[4] Although most modern studies claim that the request for Bonaventure to write an official biography was made by the General Chapter of Narbonne in 1260, it is possible that it came from the General Chapter of Rome in 1257, the year Bonaventure was appointed as Minister General of the Order. See J. M. Hammond, "Bonaventure," in *New Catholic Encyclopedia,* 2nd edition, edited by Berhard Marthaler, et al. (Detroit, 2002), 482.

[5] Hammond, "Bonaventure," 482.

[6] "Introduction to the Legends and Sermons about Saint Francis by Bonaventure of Bagnoregio," in *Francis of Assisi: Early Documents,* volume 2, *The Founder,* ed. Regis J. Armstrong, J. A. Wayne Hellmann, and William J. Short (New York: New City Press, 2000), hereafter referred to as FA:ED II followed by page number. This reference is *FA:ED* II, 503.

[7] Lazaro Iriarte, "Francis of Assisi and the Evangelical Movements of His Time," trans. Edward Hagman, *Greyfriars Review* 12.2 (1998): 169.

[8] For a historical background of Beguine women see Ernst McDonald, *The Beguines and Beghards in Medieval Culture* (New York: Octagon Books, 1969); Bernard McGinn (ed.), *Meister Eckhart and the Beguine Mystics: Hadewijch of Brabant, Mechtild of Magdeburg, and Marguerite Porete* (New York: Continuum, 1994), 1–14.

[9] Francis of Assisi, "Testament" 14 (*Écrits,* 206). Engl. trans. *FA:ED* I, 125.

[10] Francis of Assisi, *Later Rule* 1.1 (*Écrits,* 122). Engl. trans. *FA:ED* I, 100.

[11] Joseph P. Chinnici, "Evangelical and Apostolic Tensions," in *Our Franciscan Charism Today* (New Jersey: Fame, 1987), 7.

[12] Michael Blastic, "'It Pleases Me that You Should Teach Sacred Theology': Franciscans Doing Theology," *Franciscan Studies* 55 (1998): 8.

[13] Ibid., 5–8.

[14] Chinnici, "Evangelical and Apostolic Tensions," 7.

[15] Dominic Monti, "Francis as Vernacular Theologian: A Link to the Franciscan Intellectual Tradition," in *The Franciscan Intellectual Tradition,* edited by Elise Saggau (New York: The Franciscan Institute, 2001), 21–42.

[16] For a comprehensive treatment of Bonaventure's worldview see Ilia Delio, *Simply Bonaventure: An Introduction to his Life, Thought and Writings* (New York: New City Press, 2001).

[17] In the prologue to his *Itinerarium Mentis in Deum (Soul's Journey into God)* Bonaventure writes, "I call upon the Eternal Father through his Son, our Lord Jesus Christ . . . and through the intercession of blessed Francis, our leader and father, he may enlighten the eyes of our soul to guide our feet in the way of that peace which surpasses all understanding." See *Bonaventure: The Soul's Journey into God, The Tree of Life, The Major Life of Saint Francis,* trans. Ewert Cousins (New York: Paulist, 1978), 53.

[18] Francis of Assisi, *Later Rule* 10.8 (*Écrits,* 196). Engl. trans. *FA:ED* I, 105.

[19] See "The Form of Life of Clare of Assisi," in *Clare of Assisi: Early Documents,* edited and translated by Regis J. Armstrong, 2nd edition (New York: The Franciscan Institute, 1993), 64. Clare begins her Rule by saying, "Clare, unworthy servant of Christ and the *little plant* of the most blessed Francis."

[20] For historical background on Clare's life of enclosure at the convent of San Damiano see Margaret Carney, *Clare of Assisi* (Quincy, IL: Franciscan Press, 1993), 65–77; Marco Bartoli, *Clare of Assisi,* trans. Sr. Francis Teresa (Quincy, IL: Franciscan Press, 1993), 53–97.

[21] There is evidence that the privilege of poverty from Innocent III is a forgery; however, Clare may have received such a privilege from Innocent IV and definitely from Gregory IX. When she actually received this privilege, however, is uncertain. See W. Maleczek, "Questions About the Authenticity of the Privilege of Poverty of Innocent III and of the Testament of Clare of Assisi," trans. Cyprian Rosen and Dawn Nothwehr, *Greyfriars Review* 12 (Supplement, 1998): 1–80; Bartoli, *Clare of Assisi,* 9; Engelbet Grau, "Saint Clare's *Privilegium Paupertatis* Its History and Significance," trans. Sr. M. Jane Frances, *Greyfriars Review* 6.3 (1992): 327–36.

[22] Clare's four letters to Agnes of Prague are contained in *Clare of Assisi: Early Documents.* The letters are abbreviated by number of letter, *LAg* and paragraph number. The critical edition of Clare's writings is found in *Claire d'Assise: Écrits,* intro., trans., and notes, Marie-France Becker, Jean-François Godet, Thaddée Matura, *Sources Chrétiennes,* number 325 (Paris: Les Editions du Cerf, 1985). This quote is in 4 *LAg* 1 (*Écrits,* 110).

[23] Recent scholarship on the *Testament* of Clare indicates that this may not be an authentic work but rather belongs to the manuscripts of fifteenth-century Poor Clares associated with the Observant reform. Maleczek ("Questions About the Authenticity of the Privilege of Poverty of Innocent III", 78) claims that the insistence on poverty in the *Testament* is more appropriate to the time of the Observant Reform in the second half of the fifteenth century than to the years before Clare's death.

[24] Clare of Assisi, "Second Letter to Agnes of Prague" (2 *LAg*) 20–21 (*Écrits,* 96-98). Engl. trans. Armstrong, *Clare of Assisi: Early Documents,* 42.

[25] *Angela of Foligno: Complete Works,* translated by Paul Lachance (New York: Paulist, 1993), 242.

[26] According to Carmelite scholars, this prayer known as the "Prayer of Saint Teresa," has an unknown source. In a private communication Steven Payne, O.C.D., wrote: "Kieran [Kavanaugh] and I have been wondering about this for years. We've looked for a source for this text but it's not found in any of Teresa's published writings." The prayer may be a modern composition attributed to Saint Teresa.

Chapter One

DIVINE-HUMAN RELATIONSHIP

The lover was asked to whom he belonged.
He answered, "To love."
"What are you made of?" "Of love."
"Who gave birth to you?" "Love."
"Where were you born?" "In love."
"Who brought you up?" "Love."
"How do you live?" "By love."
"What is your name?" "Love."
"Where do you come from?" "From love."
"Where are you going?" "To love."
"Where are you now?" "In love."
"Have you anything other than love?"
"Yes, I have faults and wrongs against my beloved."
"Is there pardon in your beloved?"
The lover said that in his beloved were mercy and justice,
and that he therefore lived between fear and hope.

—Ramón Lull,
The Book of the Lover and the Beloved

Every person has a need to talk, to express himself or herself. Some people talk to themselves and some people talk to others. In an age of cell phones people seem to be in daily, if not incessant, communication. The immense popularity of cell phones suggests that there is a need for people to express themselves to others. Whether on a train, in a store or standing on a corner waiting to cross the street, people are talking because they have a need to share their thoughts with another person, or simply because they do not want to feel alone. One of the reasons we are always in some type of communication—a spiritual reason—is that we are made in the image of God. The great spiritual writer Augustine of Hippo captured the longing of the human heart in the beginning of his Confessions: "You have made us for yourself O God and our hearts are restless until they rest in you."[1] Prayer is the longing of the human heart for God. It is a yearning and desire for relationship with God, and it is God's attention to our desire: God-in-communion with us. Because we are created by God we long for God. In God is the source of my identity, the truth of who I am and who I am called to be. If I am to find happiness, I can only find it in God.

Prayer is not a one-sided relationship. It is not simply *my* longing for God but it is God's longing for me as well. Prayer is an awakening to the fact that the fulfillment of my life lies in God. God delights in his creation and loves each of us with a personal love. Therefore, prayer is God's desire to breathe in me, to be the Spirit of my life and to draw me into the fullness of life. When I pray, when I breathe with God, I become part of the intimacy of God's life. The Spirit of God who breathes within me draws me into the circle of love between the Father and Son. Through prayer I am drawn into the dance of the Trinity.

This intimacy of prayer—breathing with the Spirit of God—was at the heart of the life of Francis of Assisi. He advised his followers to have, above all things (*supra omnia*) the Spirit of the Lord and his holy manner of working, to pray always and to have a pure heart. Breathing in the Spirit of God and exhaling his holy manner of working exemplified

Francis' life. The first biographer of Francis, Thomas of Celano, described Francis as "living prayer." "Francis did not so much pray," he wrote, "as he himself became prayer."[2] This idea helps us realize that Francis did not recite many prayers but rather he lived in a deep relationship with God—he became prayer. Prayer is the expression of intimacy with God and ultimately must shape the way we live our lives and what we become among the living.

If prayer shapes who I am and what I become, then what I become in this breathing with God must be the source of my identity, that is, the identity of who God created me to be from all eternity. In his lectures on the *Six Days of Creation*, Bonaventure indicated that love is like a sculptor who chisels away until a beautiful image is revealed. "Love is always preceded by negation," he wrote, "a sculptor never adds anything; rather he removes matter leaving the noble and beautiful form in the stone."[3] Prayer is that love of God that clears away the dross that covers the image of God in which I am created. It uncovers something that is precious and glorious within me. Prayer, therefore, is like the birth of a child. It is the discovery of the new being within me. Since it is the most direct line of communication to my interior reality, every denial of that reality is a diminishment of myself.

Prayer that leads to the beauty of the image within is difficult for it requires honesty and humility. It requires freedom from expectations, projections, false hopes and self-centeredness. It means to be able to say, I am who I am with my strengths and weaknesses, gifts and failings. In one of his *Admonitions* Francis wrote, "what a person is before God, that he is and no more."[4] For Francis, humility and self-knowledge belong together. When we can accept our "thisness"[5] then we are free to breathe in the love of God and can go out to embrace God in the other. Prayer, therefore, requires an honest encounter with God, a turning of the mind and heart to God. When we fail in this honesty we diminish ourselves because we fail to allow the fullness of God's Spirit to move within us and thus we fail to come to our authentic selves in God.

In his book *New Seeds of Contemplation*, Thomas Merton wrote that often we prefer the false self, a self that is hidden from God and who God knows nothing about—a self that is cut off from life-giving relationships with others.[6] The false self prevails when we lack self-knowledge or when we fail to acknowledge "this is who I am before God and nothing more [or less]." The false self is the self-centered self, the self that seeks its own security and protection, the self that is cut off from God. But if my mind and heart do not belong to God then neither do I belong to God and I wander about restlessly in the world wrapped in my false self—unaware that the secret of my identity (and happiness) lies in the love and mercy of God. Bonaventure, inspired by Saint Augustine, wrote in his *Soliloquy*, "God is the One who is closer to you than you are to yourself."[7] God is so close to each one of us that even if we deny him, as the author of the Letter to Timothy said, God will remain faithful because he cannot deny his own self (2 Timothy 2:13).

In the Franciscan path, prayer that leads to self-knowledge is the basis of relationship with God. Celano tells us that Francis had to grow in self-knowledge, for as a young man he was arrogant, unreliable, a libertine and a spendthrift.[8] Only in meeting the God of compassionate love in the cross of Jesus Christ did Francis realize that he was wrapped up in a false self far from God. As his life turned from self-centeredness toward a center in God, he acquired humility before the generous love and mercy of God. The author of "The Deeds of Blessed Francis and His Companions" describes Francis praying before the crucified Christ with the words, "Who are you, my most dear God, and who *am I, a worm* and your little servant?"[9] Prayer is living into the answer of these questions, "who are you, O God, and who am I?" Francis had a desire for wholeness of life in God but realized that such love was a deepening of knowledge in love. One of his earliest prayers is the prayer for light and knowledge: "Most High, glorious God, enlighten the darkness of my heart. Give me true faith, certain hope, and perfect charity, sense and knowledge, Lord, that I may carry out Your holy and true command."[10]

Celano tells us that the path to God for Francis was a gradual process of conversion or change of heart. What enabled Francis to change was an openness to God's grace. An example of this change is Francis' relation to the lepers of Assisi. In his early youth, he loathed the sight of lepers and quickly turned away if they approached him. During an early period of his conversion, however, he met a leper one day along the road. Instead of turning away, Francis dismounted his horse to give the leper alms. When the leper extended his arm, Francis kissed the hand of the leper and gave him alms. He mounted his horse and rode away but when he turned back to see the leper, the leper had disappeared. Was this a dream or reality? Or both? Perhaps we can say that God was beginning to breathe in the life of Francis, Francis was becoming prayer, so that what was once bitter—the sight of lepers—had become sweet.[11] God touched the heart of Francis in such a way that he could no longer remain wrapped in his false self. His opening up to God became an opening up to the truth of himself—his own "leprosy" and to the truth of the other who is created in the image of God.

Bonaventure describes Francis' conversion as a movement from an "I" centeredness to a "Thou" centeredness. Francis' encounter with God became an encounter with the other, the leper, the poor and the sick. Francis came to realize that he was no self apart from the other. Salvation, as Merton points out, means rescuing the person from the individual or, we might say, it is bringing the individual into personhood through an experience of love.[12] The word "person" is related to the Latin *"per-sonare"* which means "to sound through." To be a human person is based not on *what* we are or what we do but *who* we are in relation to God, self, others and world. It means to be in relationship with another by which the other sounds through one's life. Francis became a person because his response to grace meant God could sound through his life and through the lives of others he met along the way. The core of Francis' prayer was summed up in the words: "My God and my all" (*Deus meus et omnia*).[13] As Francis entered more deeply into prayer, the more he discovered his self in God. The Jesuit scientist and mystic, Pierre Teilhard de Chardin, claimed that the acme of our originality is not in our individuality but in being a person.[14] The more we are in union with others, the more we are "ourselves" since it is the irreproducible core of ourselves that is the basis of union with others. That is why self-identity, coming to truth of who we are really are in God, is essential to living life to its fullest as a human person.

To be human is to be on the way to salvation, that is, to be brought into relationships of wholeness and healing in union with God. Prayer leads to salvation because it leads to the happiness of being a lover of God. The thirteenth-century penitent Angela of Foligno had a deep sense of God as the "significant other" of her life, the one who made her life whole and complete. At one point in her story she describes an intimate encounter with her crucified Lover [Christ] and hears the words, "You are I and I am you."[15] To her followers she indicated that the purpose of prayer is nothing other than to manifest God and self. In her view, "the more one prays, the more one is enlightened. The more one is enlightened, the more one sees. The deeper and more perfect the vision, the more one loves. And the more one loves, the more one will delight in what one sees."[16] Prayer, therefore, leads us to know ourselves in God and God in ourselves, and in this relationship we are led to true humility by which we see clearly the humble presence of God all around us.

Francis of Assisi understood that the heart is the center of life's struggles. It is the human heart that wrestles with darkness, loneliness and the demons of the false self. Francis prayed that the darkness of his heart would be enlightened, light enough that he could love more purely and deeply. Prayer that leads to self-knowledge leads to freedom of self for we begin to let go of the masks that hide our many faces. When Francis prayed to enlighten the darkness of his heart, he prayed to be released from isolation, domination, superiority and all those things that prevented him from becoming a truly human person. He prayed for the virtues of faith, hope and love. Prayer that leads to love leads to freedom, for only in freedom can we really love another without trying to possess the other for a selfish reason. How do we come to this self-knowledge that leads to freedom? We begin, according to Bonaventure, by recognizing our human "poverty" and thus our need for God, acknowledging our limitations, fragility and human weaknesses. Prayer is the outcry of the human heart for the God of compassionate love. This outcry for God, Bonaventure writes, is the beginning of the journey to God.[17] If we desire to ascend to God, we must descend into our own humanity. The "descent" into himself or herself is not a preoccupation with the self and its concerns but the desire for God. The ascent to God, therefore, begins by going inward to the core of who we are, created in the image of God. This type of prayer, this going inwards, is risky business because we are not sure what we will find wedged into the recesses of our heart or how we will confront the things that make us ugly instead of beautiful, angry instead of joyful, isolated instead of relational. But unless we descend into what makes us who we are, we really cannot make our way to God.

As Minister General of a large Order, Bonaventure provided, among other things, spiritual direction for those seeking God. In a letter to Poor Clare nuns, he offered directives as to how we might enter into prayer by way of "descent." The steps are summarized as follows:

- Return to yourself;
- Enter into your heart;
- Ponder what you were, are, should have been, called to be;
- What you are by nature;
- What you are through sin;
- What you should have been through effort;
- What you can still be through grace;
- Meditate in your heart;
- Let your spirit brood. (Are you resentful, angry, jealous?);
- Plow this field, work on yourself;
- Strive for freedom within, the freedom that leads to relationship with God, realizing that God will never force us to love him;
- Lack of self-knowledge and failure to appreciate one's own worth make for faulty judgment in all other matters;
- If you are not able to understand (and accept) your own self, you will not be able to understand (or accept) what is beyond you.[18]

Bonaventure's advice is practical and balanced. We cannot love the God we cannot see unless we love the God we see within ourselves and in others. The more we are able to find God within ourselves, the more we can find God outside ourselves. The deeper our relation with God, the greater the realization of our identity in God, that is, the closer we come to God. The more we are ourselves the more we can love others, for no other reason or purpose but simply to love them because God is love.

The biographers of Francis indicate that, as he grew in relationship with God in and through the crucified Christ, so too he entered more deeply into relation with others. He acquired a new vision of the world around him, not that the world changed, but he changed because his heart was touched and embraced by a God of diffusive, self-giving love. Franciscan prayer is not an escape from the world but an entrance into it. We become conscious in prayer of how much the world is with us and we are in the world. Francis came to see the poor and lepers in a new way, as images of God's goodness. In his *Major Legend of Saint Francis*, Bonaventure uses the symbol of the kiss to signify Francis' embrace of the leper. He writes, "after Francis was impressed with the passion of Christ he, in order to despise himself completely, showed deeds of humility and humanity to lepers with a gentle piety...with a great drive of *compassion* [he] kissed their hands and mouth."[19] Further on he states, "he even kissed their ulcerous wounds."[20] According to Bernard of Clairvaux, the kiss symbolizes the Incarnation.[21] Bonaventure used this symbol to indicate that Francis discovered the sweetness of God hidden in the bitter flesh of the leper. Just as God reached out to embrace Francis in the compassionate love of the cross, so too that same God was now present in the distorted figure of the leper. The otherness of God's love revealed in Christ created a space in Francis for the otherness of the leper to enter. In this way, Francis became open to the otherness of the leper as the experience of self-transcendence. The leper was no longer an object of charity but a source of God's loving embrace and thus someone Francis was intimately related to. Francis began to identify with the leper as brother because the leper was not simply another person outside Francis' self but the other of Francis' self-transcendent desire.[22] Growth in prayer leads one like Francis to a state where his center of gravity is no longer in the self, but in God. This "restructuring of self" results from one's experience of God's presence. Prayer opens us up to the other, that is, the otherness of God in ourselves and in our neighbor.

How do we begin this descent into our humanity, this journey to humility and freedom and to the fullness of life in God? It requires first and foremost solitude of place and solitude of heart. Solitude is not the same as loneliness. Whereas loneliness is the deafening silence of being alone, isolated and enclosed, solitude is being alone with God. It is a retreat into silence so as to be in communion with the source of life. Francis was a person of solitude.[23] "In the clefts of the rocks," Celano writes, "he would build his nest and in the hollow of the wall his dwelling...he often chose solitary places to focus his entire heart on God."[24] Although Francis physically traveled to mountain retreats (establishing around seventeen hermitages) he himself realized that physical silence is not necessarily solitude. According to the author of the *Three Companions* Francis claimed,

> Let your behavior be as decent as if you were staying in a hermitage or a cell because wherever we are or wherever we travel, we have a cell with us. Brother body is our cell, and the soul is the hermit who remains inside the cell to pray to God and meditate. So if the soul does not remain in quiet and solitude in its cell, a cell made by hands does little good.[25]

Bonaventure, too, realized that solitude is essential to prayer and spoke of the solitude of the heart. "When you pray," he wrote, "gather up your whole self and with your beloved enter into the chamber of your heart. Remain alone with him there. Rise aloft. Enter into the place of the wonderful tabernacle, even to the house of God."[26] Bonaventure reminds us that the human person is the temple of God where the Spirit dwells (1 Corinthians 3:17). How often we forget about the sacredness of our lives! How often we go about wandering in the world searching for God and for the things of God—peace, love, unity—buying up all sorts of things such as books and tapes, enrolling in workshops, only to realize that the God we seek stands at the door of our hearts inviting us into the banquet of life; however, we must open the door to receive the guest. Loneliness is the "black hole" of the soul that is unable to find God in the quiet of a hermitage or in community because the energy of life is absorbed by anxiety, hurt or the sense of rejection. The darkness of loneliness can be so great that one may fail to notice the light of God's unobtrusive presence in one's life.

To find God in the solitude of the heart, one must be obedient to the Spirit of God. The root of the word *obedience* (*audire*) means to listen. Obedience is listening to the breath of God's Spirit in our lives.[27] Listening in the silence of prayer can be a deafening experience if the forces of noise and darkness constantly prevail on us. Although Francis spent much of his time in solitude, his biographers tell us that he was often confronted by demons and that much of his prayer was fighting against forces that threatened to separate him from the love of God. Celano, for example, tells us that one time the devil struggled to drive Francis away from prayer by threatening him with an image of a hunchback woman. He writes,

> As he began to visit hidden places conducive to prayer, the devil struggled to drive him away with an evil trick. He made Francis think of a horribly hunchbacked woman who lived in town and whose looks scared everyone. The devil threatened that he would become like her if he did not turn back sensibly from what he had begun. But strengthened by the Lord, he rejoiced at a response of healing and grace.[28]

The story of the woman indicates that we cannot engage in a life of prayer without coming up against the reality of those forces of darkness within ourselves and around us. The woman in Celano's story is a symbol of everything that tries to turn us away from the light of truth. Because we are afraid of holiness, of leaving our selfish selves behind, we do not even try to climb the mountain but pitch our tents in the valley and settle down on the plain of mediocrity. Celano tells us that, another time, while Francis was saying a set of prayers his eyes fell on a cup he had whittled and he felt his inner self "was being hindered in its devotion." His deep sorrow at being distracted in prayer by the cup caused him to grab the cup and burn it in the fire. "Let us be ashamed," he said, "to be seized by petty distractions when we are speaking with the Great King at the time of prayer."[29] Prayer, in Francis' view, is so central to life that nothing finite is to extinguish or interfere with this Spirit of life.

To become prayer is to trust in the grace of God and God's love for us despite the forces of darkness. It is to persevere in prayer, even in the midst of struggle, striving to overcome the obstacles that get in our way of relationship with God. Francis' life was marked by sadness, disillusionment and discouragement. His was a contest, a battle, an *agonia*, like Christ himself went through in the Garden of Gethsemane.[30] But Francis trusted God enough not to let go of the divine embrace or to resign from prayer even in the long periods of darkness. His life indicates to us that if we persevere in prayer we will find God in the center of our lives and the bitter will become sweet; however, if we stay on the plain of mediocrity then the bitter may remain bitter. To trust in the power of God's grace through darkness, isolation, bitterness and rejection is to be on the way to becoming prayer because it is the way to freedom in God. For prayer, that deep relationship of God breathing in us, requires change and conversion. And where there is change, there is the letting go of the old and the giving birth to the new. To pray is to be open to the new, to the future in God. The way to life passes through change and ultimately the change from death to life. Prayer is the way to life because in prayer we are invited to change and to grow in love. We are invited into relationship with God who loves us and is faithful to us even when the world around us seems to fail. For it is in darkness that God's light shines radiantly. Thus we must enter into the darkness to see the light. We must enter into the center of our hearts to find the solitude of God's loving embrace.

Meditation

Our desire for God depends on how we search for God. Do we search for God wholeheartedly or is the God-search something we do in our spare time, when we are not busy? Francis desired to love God wholeheartedly and dedicated his entire life to relationship with God. Meditate on the following prayer of Francis and see how this prayer speaks to you.

> With our whole heart, our whole soul, our whole mind,
> with our whole strength and fortitude, with our whole

understanding, with all our powers, with every effort, every affection, every feeling, every desire and wish, let us all love the Lord God. ("Prayer and Thanksgiving")

Throughout the course of the day, be attentive to the presence of God in your life and consider the following:

1. Where are you in your relation to God at this present time? Are you striving for a wholehearted relationship with God?
2. How does prayer influence the shape of your life? Do you view prayer as an integral part of your life? What helps you to pray? What distracts you from prayer?
3. As you pray, try to enter into your own heart. What do you find? Do you pray honestly or do you wear a mask by presenting an image of who you think God wants to see rather than who you really are? What are some of the difficulties of honestly facing who you are?
4. Pray and reflect on the text of Jeremiah 31:3: "I have loved you with an everlasting love, therefore I have continued my faithfulness to you." How do you live in relation to a God of faithful love? What do you find difficult in your relationship with God?

NOTES

[1] *The Confessions of Saint Augustine*, translated by John K. Ryan (New York: Image Books, 1960), 43.

[2] *FA:ED* II, 310. Celano writes: "Thus he would direct all his attention and affection toward the one thing he asked of the Lord, not so much praying as becoming totally prayer."

[3] Bonaventure, *Collationes in Hexaëmeron* (*Hex.*) 2.33 (*Hex.* 342). Engl. trans. José de Vinck, "Collations on the Six Days of Creation," in *The Works of Saint Bonaventure*, volume 5 (Paterson, N.J.: Saint Anthony Press, 1966), 40. The critical edition of Bonaventure's works is the *Opera Omnia* ed. PP. Collegii S. Bonaventurae, 10 vols. (Quaracchi, 1882–1902). Latin texts are indicated by volume and page number in parentheses.

[4] Francis of Assisi, "Admonition XIX" (*Écrits*, 108). Engl. trans. *FA:ED* I, 135. Francis writes, "Blessed is the servant who does not consider himself any better when he is praised and exalted by people than when he is considered worthless, simple, and looked upon, for what a person is before God, that he is and no more"; Bonaventure, "The Major Legend of Saint Francis" 6.1 in *FA:ED* II, 569.

[5] The Latin equivalent of this term, *haecceitas*, was a term used by the thirteenth-century philosopher Duns Scotus to describe the individuation of things. For a discussion on individuation in Scotus see Allan Wolter, "Scotus's Individuation Theory," in *The Philosophical Theology of John Duns Scotus*, ed. Marilyn McCord Adams (Ithaca: Cornell University Press, 1990), 76, n. 26; Mary Beth Ingham, *Scotus for Dunces: An Introduction to the Subtle Doctor* (New York: The Franciscan Institute, 2003), 110–12.

[6] Thomas Merton, *New Seeds of Contemplation* (New York: New Directions, 1961), 34.

[7] Bonaventure, *Soliloquium (Solil.)* 1.5 (VIII, 31). Engl. trans. Jose de Vinck, *Soliloquy,* in *The Works of Bonaventure*, vol. 3, Opuscula (Paterson, N.J.: Saint Anthony Guild Press, 1966), 44.

[8] See Thomas of Celano, "The Life of Saint Francis" 1 in *FA:ED* I, 182–183. Celano begins his biography of Francis by saying, "From his earliest years of his life his parents reared him to arrogance in accordance with the vanity of the age....He was an object of admiration to all, and he endeavored to surpass others in his flamboyant display of vain accomplishments: wit, curiosity, practical jokes and foolish talk, songs, and soft and flowing garments. Since he was very rich, he was not greedy but extravagant, not a hoarder of money but a squanderer of his property, a prudent dealer but a most unreliable steward."

[9] "The Deeds of Blessed Francis and His Companions," 9.37. Engl. trans. *Francis of Assisi: Early Documents*, vol. 3, *The Prophet,* ed. Regis J. Armstrong, J. A. Wayne Hellmann, and William J. Short (New York: New City Press, 2001), 455.

[10] Francis of Assisi, "Prayer Before a Crucifix" (*Écrits,* 334). Engl. trans. *FA:ED* I, 40.

[11] The encounter with the leper is a turning point in Francis' conversion. In his *Testament* written at the end of his life, he begins by saying, "when I was in sin, it seemed too bitter for me to see lepers. And the Lord Himself led me among them and I showed mercy to them. And when I left them, what had seemed bitter to me was turned into sweetness of soul and body." See Francis of Assisi, "Testament" I (*Écrits,* 204). Engl. trans. *FA:ED* I, 124.

[12] See Merton, *New Seeds of Contemplation,* 38.

[13] "The Deeds of Blessed Francis and His Companions," 1.20. Engl. trans. *FA:ED* III, 437.

[14] Pierre Teilhard de Chardin, *The Phenomenon of Man,* trans. Bernard Wall (New York: Harper & Row, 1959), 263.

[15] *Angela of Foligno: Complete Works,* 205.

[16] Ibid., 237.

[17] Evert Cousins, *Bonaventure: The Soul's Journey into God, The Tree of Life, The Life of St. Francis* (New York: Paulist Press, 1978), 60.

[18] Bonaventure, *Perfectione vitae ad sorores* (Perf. Vit.) 1.5 (VIII, 109). Engl. trans. Jose de Vinck, "On the Perfection of Life, Addressed to Sisters," in *The Works of Bonaventure*, vol. 1, *Mystical Opscula* (Paterson, N.J.: Saint Anthony Guild Press, 1960), 214.

[19] Bonaventure, *Legenda maior* (*Leg. maj*) 1.6 (*EM*, 12). Engl. trans. *FA:ED* II, 534. The critical edition of the *Legenda major* used here is Bonaventure *Legenda maior S. Francisci Assisiensis* [editio minor], Firenze-Quarrachi 1941. Latin texts are abbreviated as EM followed by page number. English translation: Bonaventure, "The Major Legend of Saint Francis." Engl. trans. *FA:ED* II, 531. The editors of this volume indicate that Bonaventure uses the word *compassio* five times in the text suggesting more than *miseratio* (an act of kindness) or *misericordia* (a heart sensitive to suffering). Compassion (*com-passio*) has the sense of suffering with another.

[20] Bonaventure, *Leg. maj* 2.6 (*EM*, 17). Engl. trans. *FA:ED* II, 539.

[21] See Bernard of Clairvaux, "Sermon 2," in *Bernard of Clairvaux: Selected Works*, trans. G. R. Evans (New York: Paulist, 1987), 215–17. Commenting on the text, "Let him kiss me with the kiss of his mouth" (Sg 1:1), Bernard writes, "Listen carefully here. The mouth which kisses signifies the Word who assumes human nature; the flesh which is assumed is the recipient of the kiss; the kiss, which is of both giver and receiver, is the person which is both, the mediator between God and man, the man Christ Jesus (1 Timothy 2:5). . . . O happy kiss, and wonder of amazing self-humbling which is not a mere meeting of lips, but the union of God with man." Bonaventure follows Bernard in interpreting Christ as the kiss of God, stating "Christ is the kiss described in the first verse of the *Canticle* . . . since the kiss is the medium between the one kissing and the one kissed." See Bonaventure, "Sermon II on the Nativity of the Lord," trans. Zachary Hayes in *What Manner of Man? Sermons on Christ by Saint Bonaventure*, 2nd ed. (Chicago: Franciscan Herald Press, 1989), 71.

[22] Bonaventure, *Leg. maj* 2.6 (LM, 17–18). Engl. trans. *FA:ED* II, 539–40.

[23] For a discussion on solitude in Francis see Octavian Schmucki, "Place of Solitude: An Essay on the External Circumstances of the Prayer Life of Saint Francis of Assisi," trans. Sebastian Holland *Greyfriars Review* 2 (1988): 77–132; Thomas Merton, *Contemplation in a World of Action* (Garden City, New York: Image Books, 1973), 273–81.

[24] Thomas of Celano, "The Life of Saint Francis," 27 in *FA:ED* I, 243–44.

[25] "The Assisi Compilation," 108 in *FA:ED* II, 215.

[26] Bonaventure, *Perf. Vit.* 5.5 (VIII, 118). Engl. trans. De Vinck, "On Perfection of Life," 236.

[27] Timothy Johnson, "Speak Lord, Your Servant Is Listening": Obedience and Prayer in Franciscan Spirituality," *Cord* 42.2 (1992): 36–45.

[28] Thomas of Celano, "The Remembrance of the Desire of a Soul" 5 in *FA:ED* II, 248.

[29] Ibid., in *FA:ED* II, 311.

[30] Michael Hubaut, "Christ, Our Joy," trans. Paul Barrett. *Greyfriars Review* 9 (Supplement, 1995): 86.

Chapter Two

DESIRE

But if you wish to know how these things come about,
Ask grace not instruction,
Desire not understanding,
The groaning of prayer not diligent reading,
The Spouse not the teacher,
God not man,
Darkness not clarity,
Not light but the fire
That totally inflames and carries us into God
By ecstatic unctions and burning affections.
This fire is God,
And his furnace is in Jerusalem;
And Christ enkindles it
In the heat of his burning passion.

—Bonaventure
The Soul's Journey into God

W

e are surrounded by a world of desires. If one follows the commercial ads on television or in magazines, the culture directs our desires toward physical beauty, eternal youth and perfect health. The problem with cultural desires is that they can create fields of empty hearts because physical beauty is made the absolute of perfect happiness. It is probably no coincidence that a high rate of depression and loneliness today relates to misplaced desires of the human heart. To be youthful in appearance, agile in body and free of wrinkles are the desires conditioned by a consumer culture. Unfortunately, people devote time, energy and money to improve their external appearances while they neglect their interior lives. Recently someone said to me, "I have no interior life." My immediate reaction was "that's not true." Then I realized that this person lacked self-awareness, for that is what the interior life is, awareness of the desires deep within us. In the Franciscan view, if we desire happiness then our hearts must be centered in God. We must find God deep within us. No matter how many material things we accumulate, they will ultimately fail to fulfill our desire for real happiness because the life of the "I" needs the life of a "Thou."

Spiritual desire is the experience of God's presence in us or it may be the absence of God as well, since a feeling of absence may stimulate a yearning for God. It is the experience of delightful love and fearful emptiness. Spiritual desire belongs to our affective nature, the deepest center of our being—our heart—which reaches out for God. Desire is born of God because we are made in the image of God. There is something within us that longs for fulfillment and that "something" is not satisfied by anything created or finite. Highlighting Augustine's insight, we long for God and are restless until we can rest in God.

Prayer is desire. It is our affectionate reaching toward God and God's desire for us. Francis understood that the human person is "wired" for God; the desire for God is built into the structure of being human. "Desire above all things," he wrote, "to have the Spirit of the Lord and his holy manner of working."[1] That is, above all other things, desire

God. Perhaps we do desire God but we cloud this desire with other desires, the desire for riches, fame, security, knowledge and other passing things. Francis claimed that the desires of the flesh compete with the desires of the Spirit. "The Spirit of the flesh," he wrote, "very much desires and strives to have the words but cares little for the activity; it wants and desires to have a religion and holiness outwardly apparent to people. The Spirit of the Lord, however, wants the flesh to be mortified and looked down upon, considered of little worth and rejected. It strives for humility and patience, the pure, simple and true peace of the Spirit."[2] Francis did not reject the human body; rather, the "flesh" stands for everything that gets in the way of relationship with God. In his fifth admonition, which is part of a series of instructions he wrote for the brothers, he very clearly states that the body is good because it is made in the image of the Son of God.[3]

If we desire love and wholeness, then we need to take our desires seriously. We need to pay attention to our desires for they are the deepest cravings within us. In our Western materialistic culture, we tend to desire passing things, things that are material in nature—"its." But the desire that is life-giving is a desire for a "Thou" not an "it." The desire for an "it" may obscure our desire for a "Thou"—God. Thus we must be attentive to our desires and sort out their demands. Sometimes we may seek a shortcut to life's struggles and ignore our real desires. In doing so, we may cut off our desire for God. Persistence in prayer nurtures our desire for God even when there is darkness and emptiness. God is always present because God is the possibility of the (seemingly) impossible. God is hope against all hope because God is the future into which we are moving. Prayer can lead us to life when it seems as though we are in the power of death because prayer is the breath of God still breathing in us when we ourselves may be struggling for air.

We must be attentive to our desires because they act as spiritual antennas in our lives. When we find our desires fulfilled we must respond. Bonaventure tells us that when Francis heard the gospel passage, "they should not keep gold or silver or money in their belts, nor have a wallet for their journey, nor two tunics, nor shoes, nor staff" (Matthew 10:9), he exclaimed, "This is what I want; this is what I long for with all my heart."[4] The desire of Francis' heart was fulfilled in the hearing of the gospel and impelled him to change. "He immediately took off his shoes from his feet," Bonaventure wrote, "put aside his staff, cast away his wallet and money as if accursed, was content with one tunic and exchanged his leather belt for a piece of rope. He directed all his heart's desire to carry out what he had heard."[5] We see, in the life of Francis, that desire generates desire. The fulfillment of his heart's desire in hearing the gospel caused him to desire a new way of life, the life of a poor mendicant. Desires are not mere wishes. Rather, as we meet God in our desire, our soul expands. Desire enlarges our capacity for the infinite God.

For Bonaventure desire and prayer go together. In the prologue to his *Soul's Journey into God* he tells us how two years after becoming Minister General (1259) he went up to the Mount of La Verna to seek peace. While he was there he pondered the significance of Francis' stigmata and realized that there is no other path to God than through the burning love of the crucified Christ. One cannot enter this path, Bonaventure indicated, unless one is a person of desire. He wrote,

> No one is in any way disposed for divine contemplation that leads to mystical ecstasy unless like Daniel he is a *person of desires* (Daniel 9:23). Such desires are kindled in us in two ways: by an outcry of prayer that makes us call aloud in the groaning of our heart and by the flash of insight by which the mind turns most directly toward the rays of light.[6]

For Bonaventure the person of desire must go into the chambers of the heart and in the most truthful way call out to God. Prayer is the construction of our desires.[7] If desire is the compass of our lives, prayer focuses the direction. But we cannot find this direction in the noise of the world. Bonaventure encourages us to enter into our hearts, into the chambers of solitude and silence where God dwells. Here in this place of in-dwelling we can be truthful about our desires. Otherwise if we fear our desires, we may fear to pray. And if we fear to pray, our lives can become fragmented. But if we can name our desires and let these desires become prayer then grace enters in; then the Holy Spirit takes root in our hearts in such a way that God becomes intimately present, even in spiritual desolation. Prayer is where we sort out our desires and are sorted out by our desires. Everything can lead us into relationship with God as long as we keep the flame of desire burning and let this flame enlighten the darkness of our heart.

While desire is the first step to knowing God and thus the way to happiness, it can also be the root of sin. Sin is the disorder of desires. It is desire of self over and against desire for the other, preferring ourselves to God. Sin is misplaced desire. When our desires are twisted or distorted, so too our knowledge of God and self becomes twisted and distorted. If our desire is not ultimately for God then all of our desires become broken, distorted and misplaced. The research of the anthropologist Renée Girard and his student Gil Bailie has given profound insight to the root causes of sin in terms of desire. According to Girard the human person is imitative or mimetic by nature and all desire is a form of imitation.[8] One has only to watch a newborn baby to know that humans are imitative by nature, especially as the newborn follows every movement of a mother's facial expression. In his book *Violence Unveiled*, Bailie states that the story of the fall of Adam and Eve is a story of mimetic desire. It is the desire awakened by what the other has; thus, it is desire which ceases to be directed toward God. In the Genesis myth, Eve desired to eat of the fruit of knowledge of good and evil and Adam desired what was offered to Eve.[9] Mimetic desire is contagious desire that can lead to rivalry. It marks all forms of greed because it is the type of desire that says, "I want what you have." While we are created to imitate God (*imago Dei*), contagious desire shifts us away from God and focuses us on our neighbors or friends who become our enemies because of what they have. This shift, in Girard's view, leads to violence. Oftentimes contagious desire seeks to express itself not in the object of its desire but in a scapegoat, the victim toward whom one projects one's thwarted desires. Girard's reading of Scripture as a story of sacred violence led him to posit that Jesus of Nazareth broke humanity's spiral of violence because he willingly gave himself to be crucified out of love and thus became the scapegoat for all of humanity. Jesus confronted violence with the truth of the unconditional love of God.[10] Bonaventure helps redirect human desire to its proper end, to the God who is peace, by focusing on the crucified Christ. In his letter to the Poor Clares he writes: "Anyone who wishes to keep the flame of ardor alive within oneself should frequently—or rather incessantly—contemplate in one's heart Christ dying upon the cross."[11] For Bonaventure, meditation on the crucified Christ will lead to right and true relationship with God because in the cross we encounter a God of humble love. The cross can help reset the tangled desires of the human heart because the cross reveals God's single-hearted desire for us and the way we can share in that desire. Christ crucified is the mystery of God's love, the passionate love of God, and we are to find the God of unconditional love in the outstretched figure of Jesus on the cross. Here God bends low to kiss us. As Bonaventure writes:

> Christ on the cross bows his head, waiting for you, that he
> may kiss you; his arms are outstretched, that he may
> embrace you; his hands are open, that he may enrich you;
> his body spread out, that he may give himself totally; his
> feet are nailed, that he may stay there; his side open for you,
> that he may let you enter there.[12]

On the cross, Bonaventure indicates, we meet the beloved, and in this embrace of love can be found the happiness of our desires.

No doubt the cross is a strange place to fulfill one's desires, especially in view of our culture that rejects suffering or marginalizes those who suffer: the terminally ill, the handicapped and elderly. But for the early Franciscans, the cross was the most visible expression of God's love for us. Clare of Assisi, like Bonaventure, saw in the crucified Christ the kenotic embrace of God's love. The word *kenosis* means to empty oneself as Paul writes in Philippians 2:7, "he emptied himself." Although Clare does not use the word *kenosis* explicitly, her notion of God's poverty and condescending love reflects this idea.[13] In her first letter to Agnes of Prague she wrote, "Be strengthened in the holy service which you have undertaken out of a burning desire for the Poor crucified, who for the sake of all of us took upon Himself the passion of the cross."[14]

For Clare and Bonaventure, desire for God involves relationship with God. If God was simply an unmoved Mover or a remote clock-maker then we would have a dispassionate God who could remain aloof and disinterested in the events of creation. Clare and Bonaventure, however, perceive another kind of God, a God who is generous and self-giving in love, a God who is relational by nature precisely because God is love and desires to share love with another. God is Trinity because God is relationship in love. This God loves us totally and unconditionally to the extent that God shares with us the suffering of our lives. In the cross God's desire for us is shown in the outstretched arms of Jesus, his love for us is expressed in his wounded flesh, his desire for us is revealed in his gaze upon us. Without attentiveness to our inner selves, however, we may not be attentive to God's desire for us. In the Gospels, Jesus often asked his followers, "what do you want me to do?" He didn't force his way into peoples' lives. For example the blind man Bartimaeus approached Jesus who asked, "What do you want me to do for you?" Bartimaeus answered, "My teacher, let me see again." "Go," Jesus said, "your faith has made you well" (Mark 10:51–52). Bartimaeus was healed because his *desire* for healing met Jesus' desire to heal. This story indicates that our desire for God is God's desire for us. Without both desires there can be no mutual relationship and thus no healing.

Mutual desire is the key to friendship. In human relations, friend-ship is possible because of a blending of desires. If a person wants to be my friend but I am not attentive to this desire I may easily overlook his or her efforts to relate to me and thus thwart his or her desire for friend-ship. Too often relationships become frustrating because of ambivalent or incompatible desires in one or both parties. Friendship is possible only when the desires are mutual; they cannot be coerced. In a similar way, God's creative touch in our lives, which desires us into being, arouses in us a desire for the mystery we call God. However, if we are distracted by self-centered desires then these distractions distort our "at-traction" for God and we find ourselves in the midst of turmoil or chaos. Relationships often break down, but if there is openness to new possibilities, life will find new ways of growing and giving birth to new relationships.

The science of chaos indicates that out of chaos new things can happen. Chaos theory depends on open systems, that is, systems in which novelty can arise. Novel influences can lead the system into new patterns of behavior when the system is open to change. The novel influence within the system is a basin of attraction referred to as a "strange attractor."[15] The strange attractor is both within the system and yet different from the system's usual pattern of behavior. The strange attractor is a mystery in the sense that it is unclear how it emerges within the system. It arises spontaneously within the system and gradually lures the system into new patterns of behavior without forcing the system to change radically. Chaos theory can help us understand our relationship with God, especially when things fall apart. Because God is the source of our lives, God is always present to us. However, life's hurts or our images of God may cause us to fear God or distance ourselves from God. Because our desires are ambivalent and complex, our fears may get in the way of what we most deeply want or desire. In the simplest terms, God is present to us, lures us and desires a relationship with us but will not force us into a relationship against our will. God, we might say, is the strange attractor deep within us, at the center of our lives, perhaps even the source of chaos in our lives. God is strange because God is wholly other: God is the awesome and fascinating mystery (*mysterium tremendum et fascinans*). Yet God is attractive because God is wholly with us, present to us, embracing us in love in a way that we are often unaware of God's abiding love.

The Fathers of the church claimed that to be created in the image of God is to be a personal being, that is, a free responsible being. In our contemporary culture we think of freedom in terms of autonomy and independence, the ability to be a self-thinking subject independent of outside influences ("No one is going to tell me what to do!"). But this freedom is different from the freedom that corresponds to being the image of God. In the *Canticle of Zechariah* we read that "Blessed be the Lord God of Israel, for he has looked favorably on his people and redeemed them" (Luke 1:68). Spiritual freedom is covenantal in nature. The deeper one enters into relationship with God, the greater the freedom in loving God. The person who loves according to truth and is really free achieves unity with God, self and others.

For the human person freedom is the key to love, the possibility of choice and refusal. To be what one must in loving God, one must admit that one can be the opposite; one must admit that one can revolt. God creates an "other," a personal being capable of refusing him. The human person was created by the will of God alone but he or she cannot be deified by it alone. That is, we are created by God but we cannot become like God without our consent. We must choose God every step of the way if we desire to be "God-like." Just as it takes two to dance, it takes two to shape the human image into the likeness of God. The love of God for humans is so great that it cannot constrain, for there is no love without respect.

The German theologian Jürgen Moltmann states that the logic of creation is the logic of love. Creation is not a demonstration of God's boundless power, it is the communication of God's love that knows neither premises nor preconditions. God, therefore, acts according to his divine nature that is entirely free, and in this freedom God is entirely Godself.[16] We can say that God is like a beggar of love waiting at the soul's door without ever daring to force it. God becomes powerless before human freedom. He cannot violate it because it flows from his own omnipotence.[17] In other words, God created us free and cannot take back the gift of freedom he has given. Divine will, therefore, always will submit itself to gropings, to detours, even to revolts of human will to bring it to a free consent.[18] It is we who must choose God, who must attend to the "strange attractor" within us and in our midst.[19] For God cannot and will not force us to choose him. God's power is love and the power of God's love shows itself in freedom. The contemporary theologian John Haught states, "even in human relations we are most responsive to others whose love takes the shape of a non-interference that gives us the slack to be ourselves. We feel most liberated and most alive in the presence of those who risk letting us be ourselves."[20] In short, love does not manipulate or control but rather seeks the best for the other.

Taking this one step further we can say that the height of God's all-powerfulness in creation is shown in the powerlessness of God's love on the cross. If the cross signifies the height of God's relation to us, then with regard to creation we can say that God takes a divine risk. The human person is the highest creation of God because God gives to the human person the possibility of love and with this gift the possibility of refusing love. God risks the eternal ruin of his creation in order that it may attain its greatest potential—loving union with God. It is no wonder that the cross of Jesus Christ stands as the symbol of God's omnipotence, for it is, indeed, God's power to love unconditionally.[21] We are free to love God, but because we are free we must constantly choose God. Perhaps it would be easier if God simply made decisions for us— but then we would not have freedom—we would simply be puppets of God. God would be like a dictator or tyrant. But God is love and love is free. The greatest gift of the human person is not the ability to think but the freedom to love. God *wants* us to love him by *choosing* to love him. To love freely is first of all to trust our desires and to trust God's desire for us. Love requires faith in the lover and the ability to risk being in relationship with the other. Oftentimes we desire happiness and peace but we are afraid of new things because they require letting go of the familiar and entering the area of the unfamiliar. What will happen if I let go of what I know even though it does not bring me happiness? What will happen if I really trust God's love for me and allow God to direct my life?

In Bonaventure's view the cross symbolizes God's faithful love for us, and this love is the light of God through the dark pathways of life. The path to the fullness of love passes through suffering and death because it requires a "letting go." On the other side of the "letting go," however, is the "raising up" to new life. To encounter the embrace of God's love in the cross is to realize that Jesus is the liberator of our desires, freeing us to be who we are created to be.[22] For Bonaventure, suffering is the place where we meet the God of humble love, a God who "throws it all away" to embrace us in love. It is not surprising, therefore, that Bonaventure writes, "Anyone who wishes to keep the flame of ardor alive within oneself should contemplate in one's heart Christ dying upon the cross."[23] He reminds his readers that the cross is not about sin and judgment, but about the personal love of God: "He withstood all these sufferings to set you aflame with love for him, to move you in return to love him with your heart, soul and mind. We are invited to love him and in loving him to follow his example."[24] For Clare of Assisi, too, Christ crucified is the Spouse to whom we are to be united. "As a poor virgin," she writes, "embrace the Poor Christ."[25] If you desire God, Clare indicates, then you must be willing to find him among the lowly and humble, in the fragility of weak, human flesh. If you desire God, then you must be willing to suffer with him as well. God remains hidden behind the wall of the human heart, faithful in love as the strange attractor in our lives, luring us into a new future without forcing us to do so. Even in the midst of chaos when everything seems to have fallen apart, God is there in love and this love is the seed of a new future.

Desire for God encompasses the drama of the human condition with its frailty, weaknesses and self-centeredness, because this is where God comes to meet us and where God loves us unconditionally. The very notion of desire impels us to ask, if we desire God what do we desire? For the early Franciscans, a nice, "clean" God, detached from the suffering of creation was not the God that captured their hearts. Rather, they met the God of humble love, bent over in love in the cross of Jesus Christ. It was for *this* God that they sacrificed everything, assured that suffering would lead them to a greater union of love. According to Patricia Hampl, Francis "was a joyous mystic who *needed* to suffer the great pain of his age."[26] Francis needed to be with the poor and marginalized, with the lepers and those rejected by society because that is where he believed God truly to be. Celano captures something of this idea in his "Life of Saint Francis" when he writes that the God of Francis and the early brothers was "a God who delights to be with *the simple* and those rejected by the world."[27] As Hampl indicates, for Francis not to suffer, especially to miss out on the suffering of the world, was not to live."[28] While suffering contradicts our notion of the happy life, suffering for Francis meant participating in the suffering of humanity. It meant touching the lepers, clothing the poor and sharing his food with others. To suffer was to participate in the drama of the Incarnation because Christ himself lived a poor and humble life. Suffering, in a paradoxical way, fulfilled Francis' desire for God. The question is, what do we desire? What causes us to go beyond ourselves for something greater? The contemporary writer Ken Wilbur points out that many people are terrified of real transcendence because transcendence entails the "death" of one's isolated and separate self-sense. To strive for wholeness, to live in transcendence, is to let go and die to one's separate self. The dilemma, however, is that the very thing we desire, transcendent wholeness, we resist because we fear the loss of the separate self, the "death" of the isolated ego. As Wilbur writes,

> Because man wants real transcendence above all else, but because he will not accept the necessary death of his separate self-sense, he goes about seeking transcendence in ways that actually prevent it and force symbolic substitutes. And these substitutes come in all varieties: sex, food, money, fame, knowledge and power. All are ultimately substitute gratifications: simple substitutes for true release in wholeness.[29]

For the Franciscans, to desire God is to become the fruit of the seed that God has planted in each of us, to discover the root of our personal identity. When we are truly ourselves, God shines through us in the most glorious and unique way. However, the path must go through the cross, that is, a dying into Christ so as to rise with Christ into new life. There is no true relationship of love that does not include suffering and hardship. A parent knows the cost of a real relationship of love. Similarly, if we are to grow in a loving relationship with God we must be willing to make space in our lives for this relationship to grow. We must be willing to sacrifice and thus we cannot fear the cross. To enter into relationship with God is to allow the Spirit to dwell within our hearts, because it is the Spirit who joins us to Christ. Often we clutter our lives with things that block out room for the Spirit, and perhaps because we are so preoccupied with our cluttered lives, we fear the cost of sacrifice and true love. It is for this reason that we need to practice asceticism.

Asceticism is not a popular word today. It is associated with the early desert fathers and with a rigorous form of religious life prior to the second Vatican council. Yet, asceticism is important to nurturing our desire for God for it promotes the life of the Spirit within the heart. Asceticism involves the freedom of the person, a desire for wholeness and integration of the body and soul. The whole person, in both the struggle of ascesis and the tranquility of prayer is to become one with the Spirit in the service of prayer and love. A person is made altogether new by the power of the Spirit that gives rest to the whole body while one's hands are raised in token of prayer and open to display loving kindness. In the early church asceticism was popular because Christians believed if the normative salvific act of Christ was characterized by physical suffering, the imitation of Christ (*imitatio Christi*) must involve a willingness to take these sufferings upon oneself in all their physical reality. In the Middle Ages, too, a desire for wholeness meant some type of physical discipline or deprivation. Pleasure and pain were not viewed as psychic opposites as they have been in a post-Freudian age.[30]

Francis of Assisi lived a very ascetic life, fasting from food, sleep deprivation, long hours of prayer and wearing rough clothing. In his *Major Legend* Bonaventure writes that,

> Francis scarcely ever allowed himself cooked food; and on the rare occasions when he did so, he either mixed it with ashes or made its flavor tasteless, usually by adding water: the bare ground was a bed for his weary body; and he often used to sleep sitting up, with a piece of wood or a stone for a pillow. Clothed in a single poor little tunic, he served the Lord in cold and nakedness.[31]

Clare, too, was extremely rigorous with regard to fasting from food to the extent that Francis had to moderate her eating habits.[32] Although we may dismiss their practices as extreme or maybe eccentric, the reasons for their asceticism are still relevant. Francis had a keen sense of the sinfulness of the human person. He saw that many people have a gravity of self-centeredness that prevents real openness to the Spirit of God. His thought followed that of the Gospel writer John who wrote, "It is the spirit that gives life, the flesh is useless. The words that I have spoken to you are spirit and life" (John 6:63). What he sought through asceticism was harmony of body and spirit.

For Francis, flesh and spirit are in conflict due to sin, following what Paul described in his Letter to the Galatians. In Galatians 5:19–23 Paul speaks of the vices of the flesh; similarly, in his *Rule* Francis lists them as "pride, vainglory, envy, avarice, cares and worries of this world, detraction and complaint."[33] He warns against these "spiritual sins of the heart" as well as the sins of the flesh, the body and self-love. He believes that the human person is essentially good, being created in the image of God. However, the flesh is weak and is both an enemy and deceiver. Francis speaks negatively of those caught up in the flesh and those who live carnally. To overcome the spirit of the flesh he exhorts his brothers to have above all the Spirit of the Lord and its holy activity. This underscores a life of penance. In his *Earlier Exhortation,* Francis describes the life of penance as the total gift of heart, soul, mind and strength to God (1, 1), the love of neighbor as self (1, 2a) and the hatred of the body with its vices and sins (1, 2b).[34] The significance of the penitential life with the subjugation of the flesh to the spirit indicates that the life of the spirit is of paramount importance for Francis, an idea that is borne out in his understanding of Christ. Francis also associates purity of heart with adoration of God and unceasing prayer, made possible in the person in whom the Spirit of God dwells: "Then Jesus told them about a parable about their need to pray always and not to lose heart" (Luke 18:1); "God is spirit, and those who worship him must worship in spirit and in truth" (cf. John 4:24). He uses the Gospel passage of the seed (Luke 8:11) to show that only the pure of heart have the proper soil to receive the Word of God that is the spirit of truth and brings forth spirit and life (John 6:64). Only the person with a pure heart receives the Word of God and, in receiving the Word, has the Spirit of the Lord; and where the Word and Spirit dwell, so too does the Father who abides with the Word: "Those who love me will keep my word, and my Father will love them, and we will come to them and make our home with them" (John 14:23).[35] Living the gospel life as a lover of peace is the purpose of penance in the Franciscan path of prayer. In his "Life of Saint Francis" Celano states that Francis attained such harmony of flesh with spirit that "his whole body [became] a tongue" by which he proclaimed the Good News of Jesus Christ.[36]

To undergo penance brings about a profound change in our relationship with God, Francis believed. Making room for the Lord's Spirit to dwell within us brings us into a consciousness of God as the source of overflowing goodness and our vocation as children of God. Sin brings about a twisted, distorted way of looking at reality that causes us to be easily deceived and prone to act according to what seems to be immediately good or beneficial. However, penance that leads to the indwelling of the Spirit leads to fundamental human relationships that embrace a well-rounded spiritual life: a spouse united to her lover; a brother or sister doing the will of their Father; a pregnant mother who brings the child within her to birth.[37] Penance, therefore, calls us to radicality, to new relationships that mirror Christ, because through penance we are led to a single-hearted desire for God. Perseverance in prayer and openness to the Spirit are the pillars of conversion. Penance is a conscious effort to act on our desire for God. It is the struggle of conversion exercised on the tangled and wounded human heart. Although penance is difficult, it is the way we can distill the desires of our hearts as we seek to live fully human lives in which the glory of God is revealed.

Meditation

Francis kindled his desire for God by constantly striving to overcome obstacles in his life that prevented him from relationship with God. Think of your own desires and the obstacles in your life that hinder a deep relationship of God for you. The following prayer of Francis may guide you in your meditation:

> Almighty, eternal, just and merciful God, Give us miserable ones the grace to do for You alone what we know you want us to do and always to desire what pleases You. Inwardly cleansed, interiorly enlightened and inflamed by the fire of the Holy Spirit, may we be able to follow in the footprints of Your beloved Son, Our Lord Jesus Christ, and, by Your grace alone, may we make our way to You, Most High. Amen. ("A Letter to the Entire Order")

As you pray, consider the following questions:

1. How do you sort out your desires? What do you fear in your desires? Do your desires compete with one another? What competes with your desire for God?
2. At any moment during the day, what do you desire, hold and love in your heart?
3. Pray with the text Mark 10:51–52 where Jesus asks, "What do you want? What do you desire?"

NOTES

[1] Francis of Assisi, *Later Rule* 10.8 (*Écrits*, 196). Engl. trans. *FA:ED* I, 105.

[2] Francis of Assisi, *Earlier Rule* 17.11-15 (*Écrits*, 154-156). Engl. trans. *FA:ED* I, 75–76.

[3] Francis of Assisi, "Admonition V" (*Écrits*, 99). Engl. trans. *FA:ED* I, 131.

[4] Bonaventure, *Leg. maj* 3.1 (*EM*, 20). Engl. trans. *FA:ED* II, 542.

[5] Ibid.

[6] Bonaventure, *Itinerarium Mentis in Deum* (Itin.), prol. 3 (V, 295). Engl. trans. Cousins, *Bonaventure*, 55.

[7] Barry and Ann Ulanov, *Primary Speech: A Psychology of Prayer* (Atlanta: John Knox Press, 1982), 17.

[8] Renée Girard, a noted anthropologist, has described mimetic desire as the root of sacred violence in history. His ideas are explored in a number of works which include *Violence and the Sacred*, trans. Patrick Gregory (Baltimore: Johns Hopkins University Press, 1979); *The Scapegoat*, trans. Yvonne Freccero (Baltimore: Johns Hopkins University Press, 1986); *Things Hidden Since the Foundation of the World* (Stanford: Stanford University Press, 1987).

[9] Gil Bailie, *Violence Unveiled: Humanity at the Crossroads* (New York: Crossroad, 1995), 137–38.

[10] Renée Girard, *The Scapegoat*, trans. Yvonne Freccero (Baltimore: Johns Hopkins University Press, 1986).

[11] Bonaventure, *Perf. Vit.* 6.1 (VIII, 120). Engl. trans. De Vinck, "On the Perfection of Life," 239.

[12] Bonaventure, *Solil.* 1.39 (VIII, 41b). Engl. trans. De Vinck, *Soliloquy*, 69. Although I indicate the English translation of the text for those who might be interested in reading it, I have modified the translation of this particular passage: "Christus in cruce te exspectans habet caput inclinatum ad te deosculandam, habet caput inclinatum ad te deosculandam, habet brachia extensa ad te amplexandam, manus apertas ad remunerandum, corpus extensum ad se totum impendendum, pedes affixos ad commanendum, latus apertum ad te in illud intromittendam."

[13] See 1 *LAg* 17 (*Écrits*, 86). For background on the word *kenosis* see Sarah Coakley, "Kenosis: Theological Meanings and Gender Connotations," in *The Work of Love: Creation as Kenosis* (Grand Rapids, MI: Wm. B. Eerdmans, 2001), 193–97.

[14] Clare of Assisi, "First Letter to Agnes of Prague" (1 *LAg*) 13–14 (*Écrits*, 86). Engl. trans. Armstrong, *Clare of Assisi: Early Documents*, 36.

[15] The term *strange attractor* arising from chaos theory describes the shape of chaos or spontaneous movements of a system that deviate from the normal pattern of order. The use of computer imagery has helped to detect spontaneous non-linear deviations in systems that signify new patterns of order. A strange attractor is a basis of attraction that pulls the system into a visible shape. Some scientists have claimed that the appearance of the strange attractor means that order is inherent in chaos since the attractor itself is a novel pattern of order that arises spontaneously within a system. See Margaret Wheatley, *Leadership in the New Science: Learning about Organization from an Orderly Universe* (San Francisco, CA: Berrett-Koehler, 1994), 122–23.

[16] Jürgen Moltmann, *God in Creation: a new theology of creation and the spirit of God*, trans. Margaret Kohl (Minneapolis: Fortress Press, 1993), 75–6.

[17] Vladimir Lossky, *Orthodox Theology: An Introduction* (New York: Saint Vladimir's Seminary Press, 1978), 73–4.

[18] Lossky, *Orthodox Theology*, 72.

[19] Ibid., 73.

[20] John F. Haught, *Science and Religion: From Conflict to Conversation* (New York: Paulist, 1995), 161.

[21] Delio, *Simply Bonaventure*, 169.

[22] Sebastian Moore, *The Crucified Is No Stranger* (New York: Paulist, 1977), x.

[23] Bonaventure, *Perf. Vit.* 6.1 (VIII, 120). Engl. trans. De Vinck, "On the Perfection of Life," 239.

[24] Bonaventure, *Perf. Vit.* 6.9 (VIII, 122). Engl. trans. De Vinck, "On the Perfection of Life," 245.

[25] Clare of Assisi, 2 *LAg* 18 (*Écrits*, 96). Engl. trans. Armstrong, *Clare of Assisi: Early Documents*, 42.

[26] Patricia Hampl, *Virgin Time* (New York: Farrar Straus Giroux, 1992), 121.

[27] "The Life of Francis by Thomas of Celano," 12.31. Engl. trans. *FA:ED* I, 210.

[28] Hampl, *Virgin Time*, 121.

[29] Ken Wilbur, *Up From Eden: A Transpersonal View of Human Evolution* (Wheaton, IL: Quest Books, 1996), 16.

[30] Margaret Miles, *Fullness of Life: Historical Foundations for a New Asceticism* (Philadelphia: Westminster Press, 1981), 112–34, especially p. 116; Andre Louf, John Vriend, *Tuning into Grace* (Kalamazoo, MI: Cistercian Publ., 1992), 59–77.

[31] Bonaventure, *Leg. maj* 5.1 (*EM*, 38). Engl. trans. *FA:ED* II, 561.

[32] See Rudolph Bell, *Holy Anorexia* (Chicago: University of Chicago Press, 1985), 124. Bell writes that "[Francis] too was very abstemious, but it was he who ordered her to eat, not vice versa"; cf. "The Versified Legend of the Virgin Clare," in *Clare of Assisi: Early Documents*, 203 where the author writes that "for such exceptional harshness, Francis guided her more mildly"; "The Acts of the Process of Canonization," in *Clare of Assisi: Early Documents*, 154.

[33] Francis of Assisi, *Later Rule*, 10.7 (*Écrits*, 196). Engl. trans. *FA:ED* I, 105.

[34] Francis of Assisi, "Earlier Exhortation" 1 (*Écrits*, 220). Engl. trans. *FA:ED* I, 41.

[35] Francis discusses the Gospel passage of the seed in his *Earlier Rule* 22, 12–25 (*Écrits*, 162-164). Engl. trans. *FA:ED* I, 79–80.

[36] "The Life of Saint Francis by Thomas of Celano," 4.97. Engl. trans. *FA:ED* I, 266.

[37] See Francis of Assisi, "Later Admonition and Exhortation" 51–53 (*Écrits*, 236). Engl. trans. *FA:ED* I, 49.

Chapter Three

PRAYER AND THE SPIRITUAL JOURNEY

What you hold, may you [always] hold,
What you do, may you [always] do and never abandon.
But with swift pace, light step,
Unswerving feet,
So that even your steps stir up no dust,
May you go forward
Securely, joyfully, and swiftly,
On the path of prudent happiness,
Not believing anything,
Not agreeing with anything
That would dissuade you from this resolution
Or that would place a stumbling block for you on the way,
So that you may offer your vows to the Most High
In the pursuit of that perfection
To which the Spirit of the Lord has called you.

—Clare of Assisi
"The Second Letter to Agnes of Prague"

P rayer is about God and our relationship to God. The important questions we ask or the conclusions we draw about prayer center around the "God question," what we say about God or how we understand God's relation to human existence.[1] The God to whom we pray is the God who gives direction to our lives. The monastic "rule," *Lex orandi lex credendi*, holds true, that is, the law of prayer is the law of belief. If I use distant and remote language to speak of God then I will imagine that God is distant and remote. If I use male language to speak to God then I will imagine that God is male. If I use language of humility and love to pray to God then I will believe in a God who is humble and loving. The God to whom I pray is the God who directs my life; thus my image of God, the kind of God I believe in, is crucial to the way my journey of prayer proceeds. Is God essentially engaged with my human experience or disengaged? Is God primarily judge or savior for me? Do I treat God as ruler or lover? Is God faithful and interested in my world?

Kenneth Leech in his book, *The Social God*, looks at various images of God that have governed Christian belief throughout history.[2] For example, those who believe in a transcendent spiritual God who does not get involved with the messiness of the world believe that the material world is irrelevant and only truly spiritual activities are important (the Gnostic God). Prayer to this type of God can be self-centered and present peace, stillness and tranquility as ends in themselves. Followers of a God who is not passionate about creation and therefore never becomes angry or jealous promote a nice, safe God of love, life and joy (the Marcionite God). Because Jesus is a nice guy, the reality of the passion and the role of God in our ambiguity, messiness and sin is avoided. These types are like the flower children of the sixties who always proclaimed that everything is beautiful and "all you need is love." On the other hand, some people may believe that God is distant and despotic (the Arian God) and that prayer is duty and not real communication or a personal relationship. God is often in the way of everyday life because God is a harsh judge and the world is a courtroom. These people often live in the fear of God's judgment and possible punishment in eternal life. There are other images that abound as well but the bottom line is the way we experience God is the way we experience the world and all that is in the world. That is why to talk of a Franciscan path of prayer is to talk of a particular way of experiencing God.

Growth in prayer is the measure of our journey to God. The notion of journey, as it arose in the monastic tradition, corresponded to Neoplatonism, which was a specific understanding of the God-world relationship inherited from the Greek philosophers. The Neoplatonic ladder of ascent presented a movement away from the world, rising above natural, sensible things as if they were inferior and in some sense, not truly real.[3] The emphasis of spirit over matter, according to a hierarchy of being, meant an intellectualizing of mystical experience.[4] In this respect, the Neoplatonic tradition with its insistence on inner illumination and mental ascent diminished the natural goodness of the created world. Neoplatonists believed that the created world should motivate one to turn inward in the search for God. In order to know true reality one had to transcend this earthly world and contemplate the spiritual world above. The Neoplatonists, therefore, turned quickly from the material world and its individual creatures to scale the metaphysical ladder to the spiritual and divine realms by means of universal concepts.[5]

Unlike the Neoplatonists who withdrew from the sensual world in order to contemplate God, Francis of Assisi attained the heights of contemplation through a penetrating vision of creation. With a basic education in reading and writing, Francis came from a base of popular and lay experience. His family was part of the rising merchant class in Assisi. His father was a cloth merchant and owned a shop in Assisi where Francis apparently worked for some time. He was not only familiar with the daily business of buying and trading cloth but he came into contact with many different types of people—farmers, craftsmen, artists, bakers—people who worked with their hands and valued the material things of the earth. The idea of transcending this world to contemplate true reality, as the Neoplatonists maintained, would have been foreign to Francis' thinking. Rather, he regarded earthly life as possessing ideal, positive potential as God's creation. Some regard him as "the first materialist" in the best sense of the word because of the way he looked on the material world—not for *what* it is but for *how* it is—God's creation.[6]

The Franciscan journey differs from the Neoplatonic ascent because the journey to God is not linear but a journey inwards toward a new relationship with God in which God takes on flesh anew in one's life. Whereas the Neoplatonic ascent is represented by the image of a ladder, a more appropriate image for the Franciscan journey is that of the spiral, one that goes to the depths of the human person's capacity for God and the capacity of God's love for the human person. The Good News of Jesus Christ, as the Franciscans understood it, is that we do not "go to God" as if God sat in the starry heavens awaiting our arrival; rather, God has "come to us" in the Incarnation. "The eternal God has humbly bent down," Bonaventure wrote, "and lifted the dust of our nature into unity with his own person."[7] We move toward God because God has first moved toward us—this is the Franciscan path of prayer.

The journey of prayer for Franciscans is the discovery of God at the center of our lives. We pray not to acquire a relationship with God as if acquiring something that did not previously exist. Rather, we pray to disclose the image of God in which we are created, the God within us, that is, the one in whom we are created and in whom lies the seed of our identity. We pray so as to discover what we already have—"the incomparable treasure hidden in the field of the world and of the human heart."[8] We pray not to "ascend" to God but to "give birth to God," to allow the image in which we are created to become visible. We pray to bear Christ anew. In prayer, therefore, we discover what we already have, the potential for the fullness of life, and this life is the life of Christ.

Because the Franciscan path to God centers on the Incarnation, it differs from the Neoplatonic path which characterizes the monastic journey and focuses on the transcendence of God. To understand the Franciscan journey, it is helpful to understand the basic outline of the monastic ascent. Early Christian monastic writers spoke of prayer as the basis of the perfect life and the path to the kingdom of heaven. Evagrius

Ponticus, a disciple of Origen of Alexandria, said that prayer is a communing of the mind with God. One must strive for solitude of spirit so that one may be wholly attentive to God.[9] The writings of Evagrius were influential on the monk John Cassian, who wrote several treatises on prayer. For Cassian, contemplation was the object of prayer, that is, an unceasing prayer that began in this life but culminated in eternal life; purity of heart was the way to obtain this goal. Both Evagrius and Cassian held that strict asceticism and discipline made possible by a flight from the world (*fuga mundi*) were necessary to arrive at contemplation. In one of his conferences Cassian wrote,

> Therefore we must follow completely anything that can bring us to this objective, to this purity of heart, and anything which pulls away from it must be avoided as being dangerous and damaging. Everything we do, our every objective must be undertaken for the sake of this purity of heart. This is why we take on loneliness, fasting, vigils, work, nakedness. For this we must practice the readings of the Scripture, together with all the other virtuous activities, and we do so to trap and to hold our hearts from the harm of every dangerous passion and in order to rise step by step to the high point of love.[10]

The ideal for the contemplative, according to Evagrius, is to move through purification from attachment to things and sin, and to enter into an angelic state of union with God without images:

> When your spirit withdraws, as it were, little by little from the flesh because of your ardent longing for God, and turns away from every thought that derives from sensibility or memory or temperament and is filled with reverence and joy at the same time, then you can be sure that you are drawing near to that country whose name is prayer.[11]

> Monastic prayer emphasized a "return to the heart," finding one's deepest center so that one could plumb the profound depths of one's being in the presence of God who is the

source of life. Prayer as the totality of one's life meant a wholehearted dedication to the spiritual life; yet, such dedication was individual in nature. It was, in the words of the philosopher Plotinus, a "flight of the alone to the Alone."[12]

The writings of Evagrius and Cassian were influential on the *Rule of Saint Benedict*, which was the most influential rule of monastic life in the Middle Ages. The purpose of the monastic life, according to the *Rule of Saint Benedict*, is to flee the world to seek God (*quaerere Deum*), since the world poses obstacles in the search for God. The monastic life is a renunciation of one's will, the place to do spiritual combat for Christ[13] so that one may strive for the kingdom of heaven.[14] Monks sought to live the "life of the angels" through the *Opus Dei*, the work of continuous prayer that anticipated life in the heavenly Jerusalem. For Benedict, "nothing is to be preferred to the work of God (*Opus Dei*)."[15] The notion of the angelic life governed the work of unceasing prayer for monks: "Since we are already on the threshold of the kingdom and are participating in the initial benefits of eternal life, it is altogether natural that this present life be described in terms of angelic life."[16] The theme of angelic life corresponds to the eschatological direction of monastic life, that is, the desire for heaven and union with God. The spiritual writer Jean Leclercq claimed that the Jerusalem above is the end the monk strives for. It is the place where far from the world and from sin, one draws close to God, the angels and the saints who surround him.[17] The life of the monk here below, therefore, anticipates the life of heaven where the angels enjoy the vision of God.

If one reads the Benedictine *Rule*, one may surmise that Benedict had little interest in contemplation for monastic life. Rather, the goal of the life was simply to seek God. Only at the end of his *Rule* (Chapter 73) did Benedict indicate that those who had a special gift of grace could strive for contemplation, but it was not the goal of the life itself. Although the primary purpose of the monastic life was to seek God, the structure of the life according to the themes of solitude, silence, prayer and meditation enabled the monk to aspire to the highest goal of the spiritual life: union with God.[18] While Benedict spoke little of contemplation, his biographer Gregory the Great held that the contemplative life is the heavenly life that cannot be lived perfectly "in this world." Rather, contemplation is given to monks that they may anticipate by purity of heart the incorruption of heaven. Gregory claimed that the contemplative life is superior to and better than the active life and should be preferred to the active when possible.[19]

Although monastic writers flourished in the Middle Ages, perhaps the writer that best summarized the monastic spiritual journey was the Carthusian, Guigo II, who described prayer as a four-fold ladder of ascent to God. In his *Ladder of Monks* Guigo laid out the four stages of reading, meditation, prayer and contemplation as a ladder by which the monk could be lifted from earth to heaven. He summarized these stages as follows:

> *Reading* is the careful study of the Scriptures, concentrating all one's powers on it. *Meditation* is the busy application of the mind to seek with the help of one's own reason for knowledge of hidden truth. *Prayer* is the heart's devoted turning to God to drive away evil and obtain what is good. *Contemplation* is when the mind is in some sort lifted up to God and held above itself, so that it tastes the joys of everlasting sweetness. [20]

Guigo defines the functions of the steps with a decided emphasis on the rational character of the process. The careful investigation of the Scriptures requires the attention of the mind. Meditation is the studious action of the mind, investigating the knowledge of hidden truth under the impetus of one's reason. Prayer is defined in terms of the heart, and contemplation is the elevation of the mind to God.[21] The ideal of the monk was to strive for unceasing prayer, to "pray always." The prayerful reading of Scripture [*lectio divina*] and the pursuit of contemplation, together with the Liturgy of the Hours, aimed toward this goal.[22]

Although the role of the humanity of Christ played a more significant role in the ascent to God in eleventh- and twelfth-century monastic spirituality, still at the highest level of union, the humanity of Christ gave way to the eternal divine Word. Nowhere is this more evident than in the writings of Bernard of Clairvaux, whose sermons on the *Song of Songs* reflected the idea that devotion to Christ was in the service of contemplation.[23] Influenced by the twelve steps of humility described in the *Rule of Saint Benedict*, Bernard maintained that the journey to God was a movement from carnal love to spiritual love. The visible reality of Christ's life was to enable the invisible reality of God's love to be attained. Bernard wrote:

> I think this is the principal reason why the invisible God willed to be seen in the flesh and to converse with men as a man. He wanted to recapture the affections of carnal men who were unable to love in any other way, by first drawing them to the salutary love of his own humanity, and then gradually to raise them to a spiritual love.[24]

For Bernard, contemplation begins with the desire for God "here below" but finds its fulfillment in the vision of God in the heavenly Jerusalem. Union with God is a union of wills where love itself is a type of knowledge of God (*amor ipse notitia est*).[25] Other Cistercian writers such as Aelred of Rilveaux were influential on the rise of devotion to the humanity of Christ, which in turn influenced Franciscan writers such as Bonaventure, but on the whole the monastic eye was aimed toward the heavenly Jerusalem. Jean Leclercq points out that Bernard wrote more sermons on the Ascension than on any other feast of Christ.[26] Bernard himself spoke of union with God as an ecstatic union of pure love:

> But, if I may say so, let me die the death of angels that, transcending the memory of things present, I may cast off not only the desire for what are corporeal and inferior but even their images, that I may enjoy pure conversation with those who bear the likeness of purity. This kind of ecstasy, in my opinion, is alone or principally called contemplation. Not to be gripped during life by material desires is a mark of human virtue; but to gaze without the use of bodily likenesses is the sign of angelic purity.[27]

For monastic spiritual writers, in general, contemplation could only be attained in the monastery because it anticipated union with God in heaven. To strive for such union entailed a listening in silence and solitude, to be alone in the presence of the transcendent One. The busy marketplace of the world with its sinful practices, evil and contempt could only be an obstacle to the desire for union with God. It is no wonder that, up to the thirteenth century and the rise of the Franciscans, contemplation for the ordinary Christian was unthinkable. Few were believed to have the grace of this lofty pursuit. It is with the rise of Franciscan evangelical life that a new path to salvation emerged in the quest for God.

The Franciscan Path

The Franciscan path "to God" is an inversion of monastic values. Rather than fleeing the world to find God, God is to be found in the world. The idea that "the world is our cloister" finds its root in Francis of Assisi. Disillusioned as a valiant knight after being wounded in battle, Francis had a profound experience of God in the broken-down church of San Damiano where he wandered in one day. Face to face with the wounded and glorified Christ on the cross, Francis met the God of compassionate love, a God "bent over" in love in the wounds of the crucified Christ. Bonaventure describes this encounter in his *Major Legend* where he writes, "While he was praying and all of his fervor was totally absorbed in God, Christ Jesus appeared to him as fastened to a cross."[28] Bonaventure indicates that there was no exchange of words. Rather, "[Francis'] soul melted at the light, and the memory of Christ's passion was impressed on the innermost recesses of his heart."[29] This encounter with the other, crucified God, changed Francis in the very core of his being. As Bonaventure states, "From then on he clothed himself with a spirit of poverty, a sense of humility, an eagerness for intimate piety."[30] The expression of God's self-giving love in the cross impressed Francis in such a way that he began to change. This event marked the beginning of Francis' spiritual journey.

The God whom Francis discovered in the cross of Jesus Christ was, as we already pointed out, a God "who delights to be with the simple and those rejected by the world."[31] Impressed by the love of the Crucified, Francis could no longer remain alone in his search for God. Rather, he had to find God in relation to the fragile creatureliness of the other: his neighbor, his brother and, yes, even the tiny creatures of nature. The necessity of the other for Francis thrust him into radical poverty whereby everything that hindered his relation to the other was stripped away. Seeing God in the wounds of the Crucified drew Francis to a new level of compassion and to sharing his goods, indeed, his very self, with the other. Bonaventure writes that "to poor beggars he wished to give not only his possessions but his very self, sometimes taking off his clothes...ripping them in pieces to give to them."[32] The encounter with Christ as other, therefore, imparted to Francis a new openness and freedom. Embraced by the compassionate love of God, Francis was liberated within and went out to embrace the other in love.

According to Bonaventure, Francis discovered the truth of his own identity in his encounter with the crucified Christ, that is, he discovered his own woundedness in the image of the crucified man. This self-knowledge enabled him to go out to the poor and sick.[33] Describing Francis as the truly humble person, Bonaventure writes: "As Christ's disciple he strove to regard himself as worthless in his own eyes and those of others. He used to make this statement frequently: 'What a person is before God, that he is and no more.'"[34] Naming the truth of his own person before God allowed Francis to become free to make the journey to the other and back again.[35] Only in relation to the other did his weaknesses become strengths, for it was in naming his weaknesses that Francis matured in authentic human love.

Because of the mystery of Christ and the embrace of God's compassionate love in the wounded Christ, Francis grew spiritually as a person finding his true self to be a relational self. The deeper he grew in relationship with Christ, the deeper he grew in relationship with others. As Francis deepened his relationship with Christ, the other became less outside Francis as object and more related to him as brother. Community became the concrete expression of the Christ mystery for Francis. The deeper he entered into the mystery of Christ in his own life, the more he recognized Christ in the world around him, in his brothers, the lepers, in the sick and in the tiny creatures of creation. "In all the poor," Bonaventure wrote, "Francis saw before him a portrait of Christ."[36] Even animals represented Christ to him. Seeing the birth of a lamb, for example, Francis exclaimed, "Alas, brother lamb, innocent animal, always displaying Christ to people!"[37]

Bonaventure highlights the idea that the one who dwells in Christ dwells in the other, because the fullness of who we are in Christ can only be found in the other.[38] The difference of the other, therefore, was not an obstacle for Francis in his search for God but rather a celebration of God. For he found his own identity in God and he found God in the fragile, wounded flesh of his brothers and sisters. It is prayer, according to Bonaventure, that impelled Francis to see the world with new vision, a contemplative vision that penetrated the depths of reality. The world became Francis' cloister because he found it to be permeated with the goodness of God.

In his own writings, Francis showed less of a personal relationship to Christ than to the Father, the source of all goodness and the Most High. Yet, he realized that the Son is the beloved of the Father; thus the deepest reason to cling to Jesus is that he reveals the Father.[39] Francis believed that Christ alone is the One in whom the Father takes delight because the Son satisfies the Father in everything. Instead of relating to Jesus in a personal way, he often used the expression "Word of the Father" when speaking about the person of Christ. This is surprising for one who was considered a "second Christ" in the Middle Ages. Yet, we have evidence of this understanding in his own writings. In the second version of his *Later Admonition and Exhortation*, for example, he states that "Through his angel, Saint Gabriel, the Most High Father in heaven announced this Word of the Father, so worthy, so holy and glorious, in the womb of the holy and glorious Virgin Mary."[40] At the center of Francis' thought is the idea that God is communicative and expressive. The Father speaks or expresses himself and this self-expression is his Word. Jesus is the Word of the Father. Francis saw a connection between the divine Word, which is entirely worthy, holy and glorious, and the Incarnate Word, which assumed our fragile human nature. He drew attention to his followers that the Word of the Father left his divine

riches in order to take on the poverty of humanity. God expresses himself by giving himself away in love. The Incarnation is where the Word
of the Father "descends" to embrace us in love. This movement of
descent, shown to us in Christ, is a daily event that we see and touch in
the Eucharist:

> Behold, each day he humbles himself as when he came from
> the royal throne into the Virgin's womb; each day he him-
> self comes to us, appearing humbly, each day he comes
> down from the bosom of the Father upon the altar in the
> hands of a priest.[41]

The descent of the Word into humanity spoke to Francis of the humility of God. Humility did not simply mean the humble circumstances of
the earthly life of Jesus; rather, humility was another name for God who
is love. In his Praises of God he exclaimed, "You are love. You are humility." Francis called God "humility" because he perceived the love of the
Father in the descent of the Son in the Incarnation.[42] In Bonaventure's
terms, the Father bends low in love to embrace us fragile human beings
in and through the Son, the Word of God. The Word incarnate, Jesus
of Nazareth, expresses the humble love of God.

How does this theology of the Word play out in Francis' path of
prayer? For Francis, God loves us where we are with our frailty, weaknesses and insecurities. This is the meaning of his encounter with the
God of compassionate love in the cross of San Damiano. He under-
stands that while God is incomprehensible and ineffable he is at the
same time "bent over" in love for us, in and through the Son, Jesus
Christ.[43] God is infinite in love and intimate in love; far beyond us yet
intensely close to us. By following in the footprints of Jesus Christ we
are led to the Father of incomprehensible love through the Spirit, who
joins us to Christ, who in turn leads us to the Father. For Francis, Christ
is the center of the Trinity and the center of our relationship to God.

Although Francis' way of prayer, with its underlying theology of
the Word, offered a new path of divine-human relationship in the
world, it is Clare of Assisi who described the spiritual journey as one
that leads to transformation. Clare's path complemented that of Francis

but was more ordered in its direction. She had a clear focus on relationship to God and the goal of that relationship—imitation of Christ. Although Clare lived under the Benedictine *Rule* for many years, she was faithful to the spirit of Francis and his desire for evangelical life. In a way more explicit than Francis, she emphasized the Incarnation as the revelation of God and the way to encounter God.

Prayer for Clare was not climbing a ladder to God but awakening to the love of God made visible in the crucified Christ, the Spouse of the soul. It is Clare who reminds us that we hold a treasure in our earthen vessels, the treasure of God's image deep within us (2 Corinthians 4:7). To discover this treasure is to become one with the one we love, namely, Christ crucified. Prayer, therefore, is awakening to the presence of God in our lives. It is not a matter of climbing a ladder and "going to God," but of realizing that God has "come to us," taking on our humanity. Christ is the pledge of God's love for us "in whose embrace we are already caught up."[44]

One can compare Clare's path prayer to the fourfold stages described by Guigo in his *Ladder of Monks* insofar as prayer leads to union. Whereas Guigo begins with the prayerful reading of the Scriptures (*lectio divina*), Clare begins with the Word incarnate, especially as that Word appears to us in the crucified Christ. Clare's way of contemplation does not follow a Neoplatonic ascent. She does not describe a transcendence of the material world in pursuit of spiritual perfection. Her path is different from the Benedictine ladder of humility which takes the monk up the twelve steps that lead him out of the world to God. Rather, Clare's notion of contemplation, like that of Francis, begins in the encounter with the other, that is, the God who comes to us in Jesus Christ. Contemplation is not climbing a ladder but a gazing upon the other in such a way that ultimately one is drawn into the other. The gaze of the other becomes a means of self-reflection. The more one gazes upon the incarnate Word of God, the more one discovers the truth of oneself in God and, we might say, God in oneself. This type of relationship with God is not one of ascent but one of mutuality. The God that Clare relates to is a God who desires to be in full relation with us, and her path of contemplation is one of making that relationship a fruitful union in love.

In her letters to the noblewoman, Agnes of Prague, Clare describes the spiritual journey as an acceptance of the kenotic embrace of the crucified Spouse who, in the poverty of self-gift, is the beautiful Spouse to whom Agnes is to be united. She writes: "You are a spouse and the mother and the sister of our Lord Jesus Christ. Be strengthened in the holy service which you have undertaken out of a burning desire for the Poor Crucified who for the sake of all of us took upon Himself the passion of the cross."[45] Clare lays out her path to God in a fourfold manner that can be likened to the monastic *lectio divina*.[46] She advises Agnes to gaze upon the crucified Spouse and by gaze she means seeing, considering and loving the God who comes to us in Christ as she writes, "O most noble Queen, gaze upon [Him], consider [Him], contemplate [Him], as you desire to imitate [Him]."[47] We can compare her path to the four stages of Guigo:

GUIGO	CLARE
Reading of Scripture (*lectio*)	Gaze upon the cross (*intueri*)
Meditation (*meditatio*)	Consider (*considerare*)
Prayer (*oratio*)	Contemplate (*contemplari*)
Contemplation (*contemplatio*)	Imitate (*imitatio*)

Clare does not begin prayer with reading the Scriptures but with gazing on the "book" of the crucified Christ. This starting point of prayer reminds us of Francis' encounter with the crucified Christ at San Damino. In this "book of life" we are to come to know God and ourselves in God. To gaze upon the Crucified Christ is to see ourselves, others and the world with a deep, penetrating vision—to see the truth of things in their relation to God. Gazing on this book each day should lead us to ask, what do we see? How do we see? How deeply do we see? Bonaventure spoke of searching the depths of Scripture (*perscrutatio*) and, in the same way, Clare asks us to search the depths of God who comes to us in fragile humanity.[48]

Gazing upon the crucified Christ is to lead to friendship with Christ, to begin to feel what he suffered and to be able to suffer with him, in his rejection by others, in the wounds that he bears. Consideration of the crucified Spouse is to lead one to consider one's own participation in Christ's sufferings. How are we crucified? What keeps us nailed to the cross? Do we come freely to the cross or do we allow others to crucify us? Do we reject the cross and the place of death in our lives? Do we crucify others?

Consideration of the crucified Christ should then lead us, like for Clare, to contemplation, to dwell in this mystery of God with us and to become one with the Spouse in this dwelling. Contemplation is the means for discovering the truly human without disguise.[49] Clare describes the crucified Christ as a "mirror," a reflection of ourselves. The mirror of the Crucified tells us how we are most like God in this world through suffering, poverty and humility, and what we do to God in this world—crucify him. In this mirror, therefore, we see the greatness of the human capacity to love and the sorrow of human sinfulness.

Although Clare sought a unity with God through contemplation with the crucified Spouse, union is not the goal of relationship with God (as in the monastic tradition), rather, the goal is imitation (cf. 2 LAg 20). The gaze on the crucified Spouse is to lead to imitation of the Spouse. We become what we love and who we love shapes what we become. If we love things, we become a thing. If we love nothing, we become nothing. Imitation is not a literal mimicking of Christ; rather, it means becoming the image of the beloved, an image disclosed through transformation. The goal of prayer, therefore, is to be transformed into the image of the crucified Spouse. This means we are to become vessels of God's compassionate love for others. Clare's path of prayer is a deep, mutual relationship with God. It begins with the gaze of the Crucified then moves inward toward self-reflection, identity and transformation, and finally outward so that we may radiate God's face to the world. It is a "mysticism of motherhood" because through prayer we bring Christ to birth in our lives, making Christ live again.[50] Thus, it is the way of prayer that makes the gospel alive: it is prayer for gospel living. To bring Christ to birth for Francis is the fruit of penance: "We are mothers when we carry Him in our heart and body thru love and a pure and sincere conscience; and give Him birth through a holy activity, which must shine before others by example."[51] For Francis and Clare, prayer is to lead to a renewal of the "Incarnation;" God is to "take on flesh" anew in one's life through the action of the Holy Spirit, and the birth of God in one's life should shine before others, as a light to the world. Clare does not stress the spiritual over the physical; rather only when we become truly human can we radiate Christ's love to others. She stressed, therefore, becoming thoroughly human following the example of the Incarnate Word who completely lived our humanity and our fragility. In the full disclosure of one's humanity lies the glory of God.

For Clare and Francis, prayer is not a flight from the world in pursuit of a transcendent God; rather it centers on the mystical body of Christ and our participation in this mystery. God took on our flesh that we might discover his eternal face in ourselves. This is the Good News of Jesus Christ and of our lives in Christ. Prayer channels us into the depths of the Christ mystery where the fullness of our humanity and our happiness lies.

Meditation

In her second letter to Agnes, Clare directed Agnes toward relationship with the God of self-giving love. Take some time to meditate on the following words of Clare and consider whether or not your relationship with God is leading you more deeply into the mystery of Christ:

> Gaze upon [Him], Consider [Him], Contemplate [Him], As you desire to imitate [Him]. If you suffer with Him, you shall reign with Him, [If you] weep [with Him], you shall rejoice with Him, [if you] die [with Him] on the cross of tribulation, you shall possess heavenly mansions in the splendor of the saints and, in the Book of Life, your name shall be called glorious among people. ("Second Letter to Agnes of Prague")

As you reflect on Clare's words, you may also want to reflect on the following questions:

1. Who is the God to whom you pray? What is your image of God?

2. How do you envision the journey to God: as a ladder, a spiral or is there another image that captures your relationship to God?

3. Where do you find God? In silence? In other people? Only in liturgical prayer? Is God "up above" you, transcendent and distant to you? Or do you experience God's intimate presence in your life?

NOTES

[1] See Paul R. Sponheim, "The God of Prayer," in *A Primer on Prayer*, ed. Paul R. Sponheim (Philadelphia: Fortress Press, 1988), 64.

[2] Kenneth Leech, *The Social God* cited in Philip Sheldrake, *Images of Holiness: Explorations in Contemporary Spirituality* (Notre Dame, IN: Ave Maria Press, 1987), 64–5.

[3] Sean Edward Kinsella, "How Great a Gladness: Some Thoughts on Francis of Assisi and the Natural World," *Studies in Spirituality* 12 (2002): 66. According to Plato's Allegory of the Cave, which was very influential on the structure of Neoplatonism, sensible reality is comprised of ersatz forms, while the true forms lie in a transcendent, spiritual world.

[4] Ibid., 90; Ewert Cousins, "Francis of Assisi: Christian Mysticism at the Crossroads," in *Mysticism and Religious Traditions*, ed. S. Katz (New York: Oxford, 1983), 164–65.

[5] Roger D. Sorrell, *Saint Francis of Assisi and Nature: Tradition and Innovation in Western Christian Attitudes* (New York: Oxford University Press, 1988), 89; Cousins, "Francis of Assisi," 165.

[6] Paul M. Allen and Joan deRis Allen, *Francis of Assisi's Canticle of the Creatures: A Modern Spiritual Path* (New York: Continuum, 1996), 45.

[7] Bonaventure, "Sermon II on the Nativity of the Lord," in *What Manner of Man? Sermons on Christ by Saint Bonaventure*, trans. Zachary Hayes (Chicago: Franciscan Herald Press, 1989), 57.

[8] See Clare of Assisi's "Third Letter to Agnes of Prague" (3 LAg) 7 (*Écrits*, 102). The same idea is found in Bonaventure's *Soul's Journey into God* where he describes a movement inward to the center of the soul in which we discover the image of God as the image of Christ crucified.

[9] Andrew Louth, *The Origins of the Christian Mystical Tradition: From Plato to Denys* (Oxford: Clarendon, 1981), 111.

[10] John Cassian, *Conferences* 1.5–1.7 (Migne PL 49.487, 489). Engl. trans. Colm Luibheid, *Conferences* (New York: Paulist, 1985), 40–1.

[11] Evagrius Ponticus, *Praktikos* 61. Engl. trans. John Eudes Bamberger, *Evagrius Ponticus. The Praktikos: Chapters on Prayer*, Cistercian Studies Series: Number Four (Spencer: Cistercian, 1970), 65.

[12] Plotinus, *Enneads* 1.6.7. Engl. trans. Bernard McGinn, *Foundations of Mysticism: Origins to the Fifth Century*, vol. 1, *The Presence of God: A History of Western Christian Mysticism* (New York: Crossroad, 1994), 47.

[13] *Regula sancti Benedicti (RB) prologue* 3. Engl. trans. *RB1980: The Rule of Saint Benedict in Latin and English with notes*, ed. Timothy Fry (Collegeville: Liturgical Press, 1980), 159. English translations of the *Rule* are according to this edition and designated by Rule and page number.

[14] *RB prologue* 50; 73.8. Benedict writes at the end of his Rule (73.8), "Keep this little rule that we have written for beginners" indicating that if a spiritual person desires to reach after a continual vision of God, then he may pursue the path of contemplation with divine assistance. Engl. trans. *RB*, 297.

[15] *RB* 43.3.

[16] Jean Leclercq, *The Love of Learning and the Desire for God*, trans. Catharine Misrahi, 3rd edition (New York: Fordham University Press, 1982), 57–58; André Vauchez, *La spiritualite du Moyen Age occidental: VII-XII siecles* (Presses Universitaires de France, 1975), 43.

[17] Leclercq, *Love of Learning*, 55–6.

[18] Ilia Delio, *Crucified Love: Bonaventure's Mysticism of the Crucified Christ* (Quincy, IL: Franciscan Press, 1998), 190; Brian Purfield, "Francis of Assisi and Unceasing Prayer," *Cord* 39 (1989): 23–6.

[19] Bernard McGinn, *The Growth of Mysticism*, vol. 2, *The Presence of God: A History of Western Christian Mysticism* (New York: Crossroad, 1994), 74–5. Gregory's position on the active life and contemplative life is somewhat complex. On one hand he "considered the active life, fruitful in works of love of neighbor, as standing in reciprocal relationship with contemplation, so that active virtue was to foster more intense contemplation" (p. 56). On the other hand, while he claimed that contemplation is also accessible to the married, he considered the monastic life the life of contemplation and, thus, available to only a few (p. 74).

[20] Guigo II, *The Ladder of Monks: a letter on the contemplative life and Twelve Meditations*, trans. and intro. Edmund Colledge and James Walsh (Kalamazoo, MI: Cistercian, 1981), 68.

[21] Keith Egan, "Guigo II: The Theology of the Contemplative Life," in *The Spirituality of Western Christendom*, ed. E. Rozanne Elder (Kalamazoo, MI: Cistercian, 1976), 111–12.

[22] For a discussion of *lectio divina* see Gerard MacGinty, "Lectio Divina: Fount and Guide of the Spiritual Life," *Cistercian Studies* 21 (1986): 64–71; Monica Sandor, "Lectio Divina and the Monastic Spirituality of Reading," *American Benedictine Review* 40 (1989): 82–114.

[23] For example Bernard writes, "So the soul returns and is converted to the Word to be reformed by him and conformed to him. . . . Such conformity weds the soul to the Word." See Bernard of Clairvaux Sermone (Serm.) 83.3 (OB 2:299). Engl. trans. Irene Edmonds, *On the Song of Songs* IV (Kalamazoo, MI: Cistercian, 1980), 182.

[24] Bernard Serm. 20.6–8 (OB 1:118). Engl. trans. Killian Walsh, *On the Song of Songs* I, *The Works of Bernard of Clairvaux*, Cistercian Fathers series: Number four (Kalamazoo: Cistercian, 1971), 152.

[25] McGinn, *The Growth of Mysticism*, 58. McGinn states that Gregory the Great coined the phrase *amor ipse notitia est* ("Love itself is a form of knowledge"). The same idea is also found in the twelfth-century mystic, Bernard of Clairvaux, 202.

[26] Jean Leclercq, "The Mystery of the Ascension in the Sermons of Saint Bernard," *Cistercian Studies* 25 (1990): 9–16.

[27] Bernard of Clairvaux, Serm. 52.4. Engl. trans. Killian Walsh and Irene M. Edmonds, *On the Song of Songs III, The Works of Bernard of Clairvaux*, Cistercian Fathers series: Number thirty-one (Kalamazoo: Cistercian, 1979), 53.

[28] Bonaventure, *Leg. maj* 1.6 (*EM*, 12). Engl. trans. *FA:ED* II, 534.

[29] Ibid.

[30] Bonaventure, *Leg. maj* 1.6 (*EM*, 12). Engl. trans. *FA:ED* II, 534.

[31] Thomas of Celano, "The Life of Saint Francis," 12.31. Engl. trans. *FA:ED* I, 210.

[32] Bonaventure, *Leg. maj* 1.6 (EM, 13). Engl. trans. *FA:ED* II, 534.

[33] Bonaventure provides many examples of Francis' transformation into that which he disdained, namely the poor and disfigured lepers. He writes, for example, "coming to a certain neighboring monastery, he asked for alms like a beggar and received it like someone unknown and despised" (*Leg. maj*. 2.6 [*EM*, 17]; *FA:ED* II, 539).

[34] Bonaventure, *Leg. maj* 6.1 (*EM*, 47). Engl. trans. *FA:ED* II, 569.

[35] Miroslav Volf, *Exclusion and Embrace: A Theological Exploration of Identity, Otherness, and Reconciliation* (Nashville: Abingdon Press, 1996), 272–73.

[36] Bonaventure, Leg. maj 8.5 (EM, 67). Engl. trans. *FA:ED* II, 589.

[37] Bonaventure, Leg. maj 8.6 (EM, 68). Engl. trans. *FA:ED* II, 590.

[38] See Ilia Delio, "Identity and Difference in Bonaventure's Legenda maior," *Studies in Spirituality* 11 (2003).

[39] Norbert Nguyên Van-Khanh, *The Teacher of His Heart: Jesus Christ in the Thought and Writings of Saint Francis*, trans. Ed Hagman (New York: The Franciscan Institute, 1994), 149; Delio, *Crucified Love*, 7.

[40] Francis of Assisi, *Later Admonition and Exhortation* 4–5 (*Écrits*, 228). Engl. trans. *FA:ED* I, 46. It should be noted that this *Later Admonition* was formally known as "The Second Version of the Letter to the Faithful," as translated by Regis J. Armstrong and Ignatius Brady in *Francis and Clare: The Complete Works* (New York: Paulist, 1982), 66.

[41] Francis of Assisi, *Admonition One* 16–17 (Écrits, 92). Engl. trans. *FA:ED* I, 129.

[42] Ilia Delio, "Francis and the Humility of God," *Cord* 51.2 (2001): 66-8.

[43] In his *Earlier Rule* 23.11 (*Écrits*, 176), Francis writes, "Let all of us truly and humbly believe …and hope in Him, and love Him, who, without beginning and end, is unchangeable, invisible, indescribable, ineffable, incomprehensible…and totally desirable above all else." Engl. trans. *FA:ED* I, 85-6.

[44] Clare of Assisi, 1LAg 10 (Écrits, 84). Engl. trans. Armstrong, Clare of Assisi: Early Documents, 35.

[45] Clare of Assisi, 1LAg 12-13 (Écrits, 86). Engl. trans. Clare of Assisi: Early Documents, 36.

[46] See Edith Van den Goorbergh, "Clare's Prayer as Spiritual Journey," Greyfriars Review 10.3 (1996): 283–92.

[47] Clare of Assisi, 2 LAg 20 (Écrits, 96). Engl. trans. Armstrong, Clare of Assisi: Early Documents, 42.

[48] For an understanding of perscrutatio in Bonaventure see Emmanuel Falque, "The Phenomenological Act of Perscrutatio in the Proemium of Saint Bonaventure's Commentary on the Sentences," trans. Elisa Mangina, Medieval Philosophy and Theology 10 (2001): 3–22.

[49] Michael Blastic describes this phenomenological type of contemplation as distinctive of both Francis and Clare's path of contemplation. See Michael W. Blastic, "Contemplation and Compassion: A Franciscan Ministerial Spirituality," in Spirit and Life: A Journal of Contemporary Franciscanism, vol. 7, ed. Anthony Carrozzo, Vincent Cushing and Kenneth Himes (New York: The Franciscan Institute, 1997), 165.

[50] I am indebted to Delir Brunelli for the insightful term "mysticism of maternity," which I have modified to "mysticism of motherhood." See Delir Brunelli, "'Contemplation in the Following of Jesus Christ': The Experience of Clare of Assisi," Cord 52.4 (2002): 167.

[51] Francis of Assisi, "Later Admonition and Exhortation" 51–53 (Écrits, 236). Engl. trans. FA:ED I, 49.

Chapter Four

LEARNING TO GAZE: POVERTY AND PRAYER

When you have loved [Him], You are chaste;
When you have touched [Him], You become more pure;
When you have accepted [Him], You are a virgin.

Whose power is stronger,
Whose generosity more abundant,
Whose appearance more beautiful,
Whose love more tender,
Whose courtesy more gracious.

What a great and praiseworthy exchange;
To leave the things of time for those of eternity,
To choose the things of heaven for the goods of earth,
To receive the hundred-fold in place of one,
And to possess a blessed eternal life.

—Clare of Assisi
"The First Letter to Agnes of Prague"

People who grew up during the depression often speak of that period as a difficult but happy time. Whenever my mother is having a particularly lonely day she recalls the days of the depression with fond memories, as if life was never better, precisely, she claims, because people helped one another through the difficulties of daily life. I once chatted with my mother and said that maybe we should make a sign, "Poverty Builds Community." For this is, indeed, what Francis and Clare perceived in their own lives. Poverty is the basis of true relationship, and true relationship begins with God. In her first letter to Agnes, Clare writes that poverty is blessed, holy and God-centered:

> O blessed poverty, who bestows eternal riches on those who love and embrace her! O holy poverty, God promises the kingdom of heaven and, in fact, offers eternal glory and a blessed life to those who possess and desire you! O God-centered poverty, whom the Lord Jesus Christ who ruled and now rules heaven and earth, who spoke and things were made, condescended to embrace before all else![1]

The God to whom Clare directs us is not one of might and power but a God of self-giving love, a God who has become poor for us. She impels Agnes to gaze upon the God of kenotic love made visible in the crucified Spouse. This is the starting point for prayer—gazing upon the God of self-diffusive love.

To gaze is not simply to see. Rather to gaze is to be drawn into the object that one sees. We may liken a gaze to a visual experience of embrace. In his book *Exclusion and Embrace*, Miroslav Volf describes a "phenomenology of embrace" that may help us understand the power of gazing. An embrace, Volf writes, begins with opening the arms. "Open arms are a gesture of the body reaching for the other. They are a sign of discontent with my own self-enclosed identity and a code of desire for the other. I do not want to be myself only; I want the other to be part of who I am and I want to be part of the other."[2] A self that is "full of itself" can neither receive the other nor make genuine movement toward the other.[3] Open arms signify that I have "created space in myself for the other to come in and that I have made a movement out of myself so as to enter the space created by the other."[4] Volf indicates, however, that one does not stop at the embrace, for the embrace is not to make two bodies one; it is not meant to dissolve one body into the other. If the embrace is not to cancel itself, therefore, the arms must open again; this preserves the genuine identity of each subject of the embrace.[5] Nor should we try to understand the other if we are to preserve the genuine identity of the other in the embrace. If we try to understand the other on our own terms, we make the other into a projection of ourselves or try to absorb the other into ourselves. A genuine embrace entails the ability not-to-understand but nevertheless accept the other as a question in the midst of the embrace, and to let go, allowing the question of the other to remain mystery.[6]

The gaze on the Crucified Christ is an embrace, a desire to allow the otherness of God's love into our lives. Therefore it can never be an immediate vision; rather, it is a daily encounter with a God of humble love who is hidden in fragile humanity. Gazing is not simply physical sight like other physical senses that help situate oneself in an environment. Rather, gazing is of the heart by which the heart "opens its arms," so to speak, to allow the Spirit of God's love to enter. Gazing requires a space within the heart to receive what we see and to "embrace" what we see. Poverty helps create this space because when we are free of things that possess us or that we possess we are able to see more clearly and to receive what we see within us.

Gazing on the crucified Christ, as a way of encountering God, can be difficult because our modern sensibilities are not attracted to wounded bodies or suffering humanity. The daily news coverage of war and violence in the world with graphic pictures of wounded and dead bodies has made us somewhat insensitive to suffering. Culturally, we deny suffering and shun the disfigured, the abandoned and the dying. Rather, we orient ourselves to wealth, health and longevity. Yet, according to Clare, God is found in wounded, fragile flesh. In the scandalous cross we encounter the power of God's love. Clare directs us to taste this God of sweetness hidden in the crucified figure of a nailed body on the cross. We are to gaze on the face of God by gazing on the crucified Christ.

The type of prayer that Clare and Francis hold out to us—this prayer of gazing—requires openness to grace. To gaze is to be open to the Spirit of the Lord, for it is the Spirit within us who really gazes or, we might say, who "embraces" the God of humble love.[7] The Spirit who searches the depths of God reaches out for God who humbly bends low in the crucified flesh of Jesus. It is the Spirit who joins us to Christ and leads us into the embrace of the humble love of God. Gazing is a matter of the Spirit.

If the gaze that leads to transforming love is of the Spirit, then prayer must enable receptivity to the Spirit. For the Franciscans, receptivity of the Spirit means openness to the Spirit and this in turn requires a stance of poverty. We are called to be poor, that is, dispossessed, so that we may grow rich in the Spirit. One who is spiritually rich is able to love passionately because the Spirit invades the heart with the fire of love. The relationship between poverty and the Spirit in light of the crucified Christ is given different emphases by our three voices of Franciscan prayer. Bonaventure provides a theological understanding of poverty while Francis places poverty in the daily context of human relationships. Clare's stance is between Bonaventure and Francis. She views poverty as the imitation of God and the key to spiritual transformation. Let us take a look at each of these contexts more closely.

The beginning of Bonaventure's *Soul's Journey into God* reminds us that one cannot begin the journey to God unless one is poor and dependent on God: "Here begins the speculation on the poor one in the desert."[8] Without poverty, in Bonaventure's view, true prayer is difficult to nourish. The poor person is one who realizes his or her need for God. The human person is in the poverty of the desert, Bonaventure claims, simply because he or she is created. Poverty is rooted in one's existence as creature and the knowledge that one is not equal to God. Poverty means radical dependency, recognizing one's utter dependency on God. When I ask the question, "who am I?" I begin a life of poverty because the answer is one of radical dependency. I am not the source of my own life; rather, I come from God and belong to God. To be created by God is to enjoy a graced nature. However, because I am created out of nothing, I have a tendency toward nothingness. Simply by being human, therefore, I am poor because I am dependent on God for the very existence of my being. All that I have is gift, freely given to me by a God of gracious goodness. When I am able to acknowledge my poverty, I can stand before God without any demands because I stand before God unarmed, naked in the truth of who I really am. If I refuse my poverty in my desire to possess the highest good, then I will end up with nothing. That is, if I try to escape the poverty of the desert (radical dependency), I may destroy myself. If I desire a real relationship with God, a life of prayer, then gazing on the crucified Christ I must ask, do I accept the poverty of my existence? Do I acknowledge my creatureliness and my utter dependence on God?

Sin, in Bonaventure's view, is the refusal to be poor, that is, to be who we are created to be before God and in God. Francis viewed sin as self-appropriation. First, we grab for ourselves what belongs to God and to our neighbor (who is created as image of God), and then after taking what rightfully belongs to others, we exalt ourselves over and against God and neighbor. Bonaventure described sin as a turning from God and toward others.[9] This idea of turning from God is profound. It is as if God's grace holds us straight, facing in the right direction. However, because God gives us the freedom to choose to love him (because God wants us to freely love him rather than to force us to love him), we have a tendency to turn away and lose our direction. When we turn from God we become blinded in our intellect, entangled in endless questions, wandering about in the world looking for what we have lost.[10] We become caught up within ourselves and with ourselves. When we go to prayer preoccupied and entangled in our self-concerns, we have a difficult time gazing on the God who comes to us in love because we are not free to encounter God. There is no space within us to embrace God, nor can we see God in the fragile flesh of the crucified Christ because we are ensnared within our own wounds or self-centeredness. Only poverty can release us from self-concern and allow the God of crucified love to enter in.

In a culture that essentially rejects poverty, it seems ludicrous to speak of a "model of poverty"; yet, the model of poverty for Bonaventure is the crucified Christ. In Bonaventure's view the life of Jesus in its concrete form of poverty is a manifestation of the humility of God's love. The mystery of the cross is the mystery of poverty because here God is not possessing but fully communicating the mystery of his love in radical openness to and acceptance of humanity. Poverty becomes manifest in the historical career of Jesus and is expressed in the naked figure on the cross who invites us to follow him, placing our absolute trust in God alone. The Son accepts the poverty of the human condition to show that equality with God is not something to be grasped at (Philippians 2:6).[11] Bonaventure sees in poverty the renewal of the innocence and freedom of paradise. Poverty returns one to original innocence because it is fulfillment of the new law that does not promise temporal goods but love. Poverty, therefore, God's poverty, is an overflowing of love. This is how Bonaventure describes the mystery of the crucified Christ in his work *On the Perfection of Life*:

> No sorrow was ever comparable to Yours, O Lord Jesus Christ! Your blood was shed so abundantly that Your whole body was soaked with it. Not just a drop, O good Jesus, most sweet Lord! But a welling stream of blood sprang from five parts of Your body: the hands and feet in the crucifixion, the head in the crowning of thorns, the whole body in the flagellation, and the heart in the opening of Your side. Not an ounce of blood could have possibly remained in Your veins. Tell me, I beg You, most beloved Lord: why did you let Your blood pour forth in a river when a single drop would have sufficed for the redemption of the world? I know, Lord, I know in all truth that You did this for no other reason than to show the depth of Your love for me![12]

Poverty is expressed in the language of love. The crucified Word of God is the fullest expression of God's poverty and, therefore, God's love. Because revelation is the movement of God to poverty, the cross is the key to understanding God as love. No one can find God except through the poverty of the cross.

We do not usually associate poverty with power, yet, the poverty of God's love is the power of God's love. To define God's power in terms of poverty defies our conventional ideas of God as all-powerful, all-knowing and immutable. But the power of God is not brute force or domination; it is the power of unconditional love. Power is the ability to persuade. Walter Kasper writes that "only an almighty love can give itself wholly to the other and be a helpless love. Only God who is omnipotent can give himself away and yet take himself back in the giving to preserve the independence and freedom of the recipient."[13] God is the omnipotence of love because God can, in a sense, indulge in the weakness of love without perishing. It is precisely in the poverty of love that God shows himself to be a God of freedom and compassion. When we encounter Jesus on the cross, we encounter the God of infinite love who desires to share his love with a created, finite other—us. The cross symbolizes God's nearness and fidelity to us. God gives himself entirely to us in the mystery of Christ crucified in a way that, on the cross, God gazes on us like a helpless infant. Jesus is the fullest expression of God's gift to us and we are asked to gaze upon this gift and to make space for it within us, so that we may embrace the gift of God's goodness in the center of our lives and ultimately share it with others.

Francis wanted his followers to live in poverty by confidently making known their needs to one another. In his *Earlier Rule* he wrote: "Let each one confidently make known his need to the other, for if a mother loves and cares for her son according to the flesh, how much more diligently must someone love and care for his brother according to the Spirit."[14] Poverty, for Francis, was the key to love. Although poverty played a central role in his way of life, it is interesting that he almost never explains it in his writings. Francis was not really interested in the poverty of material possessions; rather he was concerned for the type of poverty that would lead to interdependence and the love of the brothers for one another. Thus he advocated that his followers live *sine proprio*—not without things but without possessing things, for when we possess things we may think that we do not need other people or have a responsibility of love toward them. Francis had profound insight into the human person and he placed poverty in the context of human relationships. Three areas where he speaks of living *sine proprio* are: 1) our inner selves and what we possess for ourselves; 2) our relationships with others and what we possess in relation to others; and 3) our relationship to God and what we possess in relation to God.[15] In all three areas Francis asked of his followers to "hold back nothing of yourselves for yourselves, so that he who gives himself totally to you may receive you totally."[16]

To live as poor persons, for Francis, is to love one another as family, as a mother loves and cares for her son. The poor person is the brother or sister who lives in dependence on others, following the poor Christ. Poverty is being able to say, "I need you," that is, "I am incomplete without you." When Jesus asked Peter, "Peter, do you love me?" he was not looking for an exchange of goods but a commitment of fidelity. When Peter exclaimed, "you know I love you!" Jesus said "when you were younger, you used to fasten your own belt and to go wherever you wished. But when you grow old, you will stretch out your hands, and someone will fasten the belt around you and take you where you do not wish to go" (John 21:17–18). Poverty is being able to have someone else put a belt around me and lead me to places I may never have thought of or may have preferred not to go. It is to be open and free to follow where God is leading, not only in my own life but in my brothers and sisters in whom God dwells.

Only relationships of poverty and humility, in Francis' view, can undo the injustices of the self-centered person. Only when we are dependent on another can we renounce autonomy and accept the gift of the other in whom God lives. Existential poverty, the poverty of being created, underlies structures of justice because it forms structures of interdependency by which all share in the common good. But to really live poverty we must ask, how much am I willing to let go? How much can I trust my neighbors, my brothers and sisters? Can I accept God's goodness in the neighbor who is different from me? Poverty, therefore, relates to our humanity; material poverty is only sacramental of the deeper poverty of being human. Poverty is to help make us human, and to be a human person is to be dependent on another; it is to be an instrument of otherness by which the other shines through in one's life. There is no sense in giving away all of my material possessions if this act does not lead me to a poverty of being interdependent, to accepting goodness from another, and to accepting the other as the goodness of God. Only care for another, in Francis' view, truly humanizes life.

For Francis, poverty was not simply a privileged evangelical virtue; it was a life of complete self-abandonment and unreserved surrender to the mercy and grace of God. Poverty led him to rest in God, meditate on God, fear God and realize a heart full of mercy.[17] Francis did not pursue poverty for its own sake but for the sake of achieving a total union with God. Material dispossession (outer poverty) led him to an inner poverty whereby Francis found himself related to everything because he realized that everything in creation shares in the same primordial goodness. In his *Major Legend of Francis* Bonaventure wrote, "When he considered the primordial source of all things, he was filled with even more abundant piety, calling creatures, no matter how small, by the name of brother or sister, because he knew they had the same source as himself."[18] Poverty constituted the core of all reality for Francis.[19] It opened his eyes to the interconnectednesss of all things in God and his dependence even on the created world.[20] Poverty, according to Francis, is the sister of humility. When we are dispossessed of things we are free to turn to the other in love. We no longer have to place ourselves over and above the other because to be humble is to know ourselves before God. Humility is related to poverty because when we can accept the truth of who we are and recognize that everything we have is gift, then we are free to give ourselves away in love.[21]

The emphasis on poverty in Clare's letters to Agnes shows that poverty is key to spiritual transformation. For Clare, poverty is related to love and to the perfection of love that is beauty. Poverty underlies the freedom within the heart to gaze upon the Spouse and to embrace the Spouse within. In this way, poverty makes room for love and love makes us beautiful because it makes us like Christ. Love removes all that hinders the beauty of God's image within us, transforming us into the presence of the living God. Clare seems to grapple with the fact that the human person has the capacity for God but is thwarted in this capacity because of sin or brokenness. "Is it not clear," she writes, "that the soul of the faithful person is greater than heaven itself?"[22] This capacity for God, she indicates, can only be realized by following Christ in poverty and humility.[23] Pride, she writes, leads to self-deception: "How many kings and queens of this world let themselves be deceived! For even though their pride may reach the skies and their heads through the clouds, in the end they are as forgotten as a dung-heap!"[24] Self-centeredness, in Clare's view, is overcome through poverty which, she claims, is the highest priority of the Christian vocation. She fought for the "privilege of poverty" and, after a long battle, won this privilege at the end of her life.

Like Francis, Clare viewed divine revelation as the movement of God to poverty shown in the life of Christ. When we become poor we become dispossessed of all that prevents us from being truly human, and it is in becoming truly human that the glory of God is revealed. To penetrate the truth of this reality, we must first penetrate the truth of who we are with our fragile tendencies and weaknesses. The mirror of the Crucified Christ tells us how we are most like God in this world through suffering, poverty and humility. The Crucified Christ also tells us of what we do to God in this world everyday—crucify him. In the mirror of the Crucified, therefore, we see the greatness of the human capacity to love and the sorrow of human sinfulness. If prayer begins with the gaze on the crucified Spouse, it must also lead us to the truth of ourselves in God.

Poverty is the organizing principle of Clare's theology, whereas beauty is the goal of spiritual transformation. Just as poverty is not a popular goal in a culture of materialism, so too poverty is rarely associated with beauty, which we associate with physical appearance. Yet, for Clare, poverty would have no meaning were it not related to divine love and beauty. In the poverty of the crucified Spouse she saw the brilliance of God's beauty, not the beauty of physical appearance but the beauty that radiates from the harmony of love. Poverty enabled her to forge a path of relationship with God by way of dispossessiveness.

Being free of everything that might clutter up her life, Clare was able to see the beauty of God's face reflected in her poor Crucified Spouse. These three ideals—poverty, beauty and transformation—form the matrix of Clare's theology and interpenetrate in the mystery of Christ crucified.[25] The poor person who is open to the Spirit of God is free to love, and the way one loves reflects the beauty of God in the world, for love is the form of God's beauty.

In light of Bonaventure, Francis and Clare, we can say that poverty is our movement into God. We cannot really gaze on the crucified Christ unless we are poor persons. The poor person is not the one vowed to poverty but the one in need of union with God, the beggar in the spirit who finds himself or herself in the desert far from his or her home.[26] According to Bonaventure, the poor cry out for mercy in the midst of misery because it is the only alternative to spiritual death.[27] Anyone who has ever prayed with the poor, that is, the economically poor, has probably witnessed the power of gazing on the God of love. The poor often pray with their whole heart and soul, with their whole being. They reveal an openness to God because they realize their dependence on God and are not afraid to share their lives with God. The poor hear the gospel with different ears and approach God with a different attitude. They teach us that true prayer is difficult to nourish without dependency on God.

To pray as a poor person is counter-cultural. To gaze on a God who is poor and humble is disarming. But if we desire to come to the full potential of our humanity so that we may know the truth of ourselves and the world in which we live then we must strive to be poor. Poverty in prayer is difficult but if we gaze daily upon the God of descending love, the God who comes to us in poverty and humility, then we can begin to be detached from the multiplicity of things in our lives and move toward the simplicity of the gaze. For the prayer of gazing means that God becomes less an idol of our own projections (needs and desires) and more of an icon of infinite love piercing through finite reality.[28] Poverty invites us to go beyond ourselves, by taking from us everything on which we might tend to lean. It is not a matter of simply being poor but of having nothing that can prevent us from being wholly open to the grace of God. The practice of poverty, therefore, is the condition and sign of our openness to the mystery of God.

Poverty must be the starting point of detachment not only from outward possessions but also from inward ones. Although becoming poor is difficult in the initial stages of the journey to God, after a while it is no longer I who put myself into a state of material or spiritual poverty so as to encounter God. Rather, it is God himself who divests me of all that I had conceived when I set out in search of him. The very activity of the Spirit of God within me strips me of all my powers— God himself shapes me as a poor person. The further I advance onto divine ground, therefore, the more I feel poverty-stricken and disarmed, and it is to this profound poverty that God calls me.[29] The experience of poverty flourishes when prayer attains its fullest point and when I realize I do not live by the power of my own life but by that of God. God's life then becomes my life, God's glory my glory. The goal of all prayer is to reach this level of union with God. It involves a stance of total receptivity to God whereby God is allowed to be "all in all," where life is experienced as pure gift and where God's goodness is felt in the depths of my being to which I must respond with gratitude and praise.[30]

Poverty is that which allows me to become fully human, to become a person in the truest sense of relationship. It is the privileged existential position in which all aspects of reality are brought to an essential fullness of being. Poverty opens the window of my heart to the love of the Holy Spirit, and it is this love that unveils the beauty of the divine image within me. By gazing upon the Crucified Christ I am led not only to the poverty of being human, but to recognize the truth of my being and my smallness in relation to God's infinite greatness and love. When I can stand before God without demands and open hands, when I can gaze on the cross and see the God of infinite love bent over to embrace me, when I learn that poverty is the language of love, then I can begin to see this humble God more deeply in the concrete, ordinary things of my life; then I can begin to see God hidden in the fragile flesh of every human person I encounter, in every creature and every aspect of creation I gaze upon. Then I can begin to be a sister to every person, to all of creation because then I will recognize my dependency on God and others. Poverty begins with my desire for God, recognizing my need for God and my heart's openness to grace. Gazing—receptivity to God—is accepting God in the other, thus transcending my judgments and self-concerns. Poverty frees me from possessing my individual thoughts and allows me to gaze on the other, thus delighting in the ways God comes into my life. "Vain it is to love the wealth we have," Bonaventure wrote, "dangerous to love that which we do not have; painful, to have that which we do not love."[31] To live *sine proprio*, to live in the poverty of being human, is to be on the way to God. Poverty creates a space within me so that God may be born anew.

Meditation

Take time today to reflect on your life as a poor person or whether or not you have considered the poverty of your humanity. Then meditate on God's poverty by reflecting on the words of Clare:

> O blessed poverty, who bestows riches on those who love and embrace her! O holy poverty, God promises the kingdom of heaven and, in fact, offers eternal glory and a blessed life to those who possess and desire you! ("First Letter to Agnes of Prague")

How does Clare's insight into the mystery of God as poor and humble love speak to you? How will this lead you to a new level of relationship with God and others? Because poverty is so integral to the Franciscan path to God, it requires continuous reflection.

Spend some time each day considering the following questions:

1. Do you accept the poverty of your existence? Do you acknowledge your creatureliness and utter dependence on God?
2. If God is near, what do you fear? If the richness of your life depends on the poverty of God's love, then what prevents you from being in real relationship with God?
3. Why is it difficult for you to become poor?
4. Meditate on Philippians 2:5–11. To what or to whom do you cling?

NOTES

[1] Clare of Assisi, 1 *LAg* 15–17 (*Écrits*, 86). Engl. trans. Armstrong, *Clare of Assisi: Early Documents*, 36.

[2] Volf, *Exclusion and Embrace*, 141.

[3] Ibid., 141.

[4] Ibid., 142.

[5] Ibid., 144.

[6] For an explanation of embrace and not-understanding see Volf, *Exclusion and Embrace*, 145–56.

[7] See Francis of Assisi's *Admonition One* in which he describes the Spirit's receptivity to the truth of Christ.

[8] See the prologue to Bonaventure's *Itinerarium Mentis in Deum*: "Incipit speculation pauperis in deserto" (V, 295). Engl. trans. Cousins, *Bonaventure*, 53.

[9] Bonaventure describes sin in the introduction to his second book on the *Sentences*. See II *Sent.* proemium; Timothy Johnson, *Bonaventure: Mystic of God's Word* (New York: New City Press, 1999), 59–64; Ibid., *The Soul in Ascent: Bonaventure on Poverty, Prayer and Union with God* (Quincy, IL: Franciscan Press, 2000), 14–23.

[10] Bonaventure, II *Sent.* proem. (II, 5–6).

[11] J. A. Wayne Hellmann, "Poverty: The Franciscan Way to God," *Theology Digest* 22 (1974): 341.

[12] Bonaventure, *Perf. Vit.* 6.6 (VIII, 122). Engl. trans. De Vinck, "On the Perfection of Life," 243.

[13] Walter Kasper, *The God of Jesus Christ*, trans. Matthew O'Connell (New York: Crossroad, 1999), 194–95.

[14] Francis of Assisi, *Later Rule* 6.8 (*Écrits*, 190). Engl. trans. *FA:ED* I, 103.

[15] For a good discussion on Francis and poverty see Regis J. Armstrong, *Saint Francis of Assisi* (New York: Crossroad, 1994), 154–65.

[16] Francis of Assisi, "A Letter to the Entire Order" 29 (*Écrits*, 250). Engl. trans. *FA:ED* I, 118.

[17] Armstrong, *Saint Francis of Assisi*, 111.

[18] Bonaventure, *Leg. maj.* 8.6. Engl. trans. *FA:ED* II, 590.

[19] John Grygus, "Poverty and Prayer: the Franciscan Way to God," *Cord* 39 (1989): 47.

[20] In his "Remembrance of the Desire of a Soul," Thomas Celano describes Francis' reverence for nature and says, "Truly, that fountain-like goodness, which will be all in all, already shone clearly in all for this saint," indicating that Francis saw God's goodness throughout all of creation. See *FA:ED* II, 354.

[21] Although Francis does not explicitly say that poverty led him to realize that all is gift, he begins his "Testament" by saying that "The Lord gave me…to begin doing penance." He then continues saying that in all aspects of his life "the Lord gave me," indicating that he perceived all to be gift. See Francis of Assisi, "Testament" 1 (Écrits, 204) in FA:ED I, 124–27.

[22] Clare of Assisi, 3 LAg 21 (Écrits, 104). Engl. trans. Armstrong, Clare of Assisi: Early Documents, 46.

[23] Clare of Assisi, 3 LAg 25 (Écrits, 106). Engl. trans. Armstrong, Clare of Assisi: Early Documents, 46.

[24] Clare of Assisi, 3 LAg 27-8 (Écrits, 106). Engl. trans. Armstrong, Clare of Assisi: Early Documents, 47. Francis of Assisi had similar admonitions to his followers. See, for example, his Admonition 7 in FA:ED I, 132.

[25] For the relationship between poverty and beauty in Clare's writings see Ilia Delio, "Clare of Assisi: Beauty and Transformation," Studies in Spirituality 10 (2002): 68–81.

[26] Saint Bonaventure's, The Mind's Journey into God, intro. and trans. Philotheus Boehner, vol. II, Works of Saint Bonaventure, ed. Philotheus Boehner and Sr. M. Frances Laughlin (New York: The Franciscan Institute, 1956), 109.

[27] Johnson, Soul in Ascent, 23.

[28] This notion of gazing resonates with some postmodern thinkers today, especially those who are trying to move beyond onto-theology. For a discussion on God as idol or icon, see Jean Luc Marion, God Without Being, trans. Thomas A. Carlson (Chicago: University of Chicago Press, 1991), 7–11; Xavier John Seubert, "Sacramentality—Icon or Idol?" in Franciscan Identity and Postmodern Culture, edited by Kathleen A. Warren (New York: The Franciscan Institute, 2002), 73–94.

[29] Yves Raguin, "Poverty and Prayer," Contemplative Review 19 (1986): 34.

[30] Grygus, "Poverty and Prayer," 47.

[31] Bonaventure, Perf. Vit. 3.9 (VIII, 114). Engl. trans. De Vinck, "On the Perfection of Life," 226.

Chapter Five

FRIENDSHIP WITH CHRIST

Christ on the cross bows his head,
Waiting for you,
That he may kiss you;
His arms are outstretched,
That he may embrace you,
His hands are open,
That he may enrich you;
His body spread out,
That he may give himself totally;
His feet are nailed,
That he may stay there;
His side is open for you,
That he may let you enter there.

—Bonaventure
Soliloquy

Recently, I was in a store thumbing through books when I noticed a small pamphlet entitled "Becoming God's Friend." I leafed through it to discover a series of meditation points on how to develop friendship with God. Although some of the points were inspiring, the book on the whole seemed to be trying to present itself as a sure method to attain friendship with God, sort of a "guaranteed or your money back" type. The Franciscan path to friendship with God is, in some ways, much more simple than a series of points but much more profound because it requires a wholehearted relationship with God. The key to friendship is in relationship, not as a point of meditation, but as a way of life. Turning one's heart toward God and centering it in God is the basis of friendship with God, that is, the God who comes to share life with us in the person of Jesus Christ. When Clare of Assisi advised Agnes of Prague to consider the Spouse to whom she had dedicated her life, she was asking Agnes to become a friend of the crucified Christ. How does prayer foster our friendship with Christ? It does so by fostering fidelity to relationship with Christ, and in this fidelity, a growing capacity for mutuality. Clare tells Agnes to "consider him." By this she means dwell on the mystery of the Incarnate Word who suffered and was crucified out of love for us. Taste the hidden sweetness of God in this mystery; feel what his friends feel; experience the love of God hidden in the flesh that was scourged, bruised and beaten. How difficult is the gaze that leads to friendship with God! But Clare is not superficial in her directives to Agnes. She is not asking Agnes to gaze and consider the crucified Christ, as if looking on a painting. Rather, she is asking Agnes to be drawn into what she sees and to become transformed in the one she loves.

Clare describes the image of the crucified Christ as a "mirror" and she advises Agnes to see herself in the mirror. The word "mirror" (*speculum*) means "reflection," "speculation," "contemplation" or "consideration."[1] It is a very feminine symbol and one that was popular among women religious in the Middle Ages. For Clare, Christ is the mirror in which God reveals himself to us and we are revealed to ourselves as we begin to see the truth of who we are—our identity—in the mirror of the cross. She writes: "Place your mind before the mirror of eternity! Place your soul in the brilliance of glory! Place your heart in the figure of the divine substance! And transform your entire being into the image of the Godhead itself through contemplation. So that you too may feel what his friends feel."[2] By asking Agnes to transform her entire being into the image of the Godhead itself, she indicates that the image in which we are created—our mind, soul and heart—is reflected in the mirror of the Crucified. In the image of the crucified Christ is the image of our human God-likeness which is the capacity to love by way of self-gift. To live in this image is to become one with the one we love. "Love him totally who gave himself totally for your love," Clare writes.[3] To live in the image of the mirror is to be transformed in the image, bearing the crucified Christ in one's own body. Clare continues in her advice to Agnes: "By following in his footprints of poverty and humility, you can always carry him spiritually in your body....And you will hold him by whom you and all things are held together."[4]

Like Clare, Francis too was a friend of Christ because he bore the marks of Christ's cross and therefore became Christ's friend, conformed to his likeness. Describing Francis as a friend of Christ, Bonaventure writes, "The Lord calls the humble his friends."[5] In Bonaventure's view, humility is a prerequisite for friendship with Christ. We must sit at the lowest place of the table of life if we are to be invited into friendship with Christ. Friendship with Christ is a grace, an invitation to enter into union with God. In the gospel of the banquet we read, "friend, go up higher." According to Bonaventure, Francis was a faithful friend of the Lord because he chose to sit in the lowest place.[6] He sought no glory for himself in this world but rather saw himself as a sinner, "an ignorant and unlearned" (*simplex et idiota*) person.[7] He was a congenial friend of God because he strove for purity of heart through penance and patience in his trials, and he was an intimate friend because he was conformed to Christ by the Stigmata. As Christ's friend, Francis was made like him in appearance by having the marks of the crucified body of Christ imprinted visibly on his own.[8]

If Francis was truly a friend of Christ, as Bonaventure claimed, then to be a friend of Christ is to be willing to love like Christ, with compassionate love for others. In his "Instructions to the Novices," Bonaventure indicates that the love of God is not a speculative idea, it is not abstract. It is real and concrete and it is shown to us in the figure of Jesus on the cross. He writes,

> Prayer is the ladder on which Jacob saw the angels of God ascending and descending. So once a day, separate yourself and call to mind the many blessings of God with deep humility of heart. Remember for your sake, he willed to be born, suffer, and die. Picture the bloody sweat, the outrageous blows, the stinging lashes, the thorny crown, the blasphemous spit, the mocking words. Picture him hanging from the cross, the bloodshot eyes, the pallid lips, the bowed head, the agony of death. No need for more. Life itself has died for us![9]

We don't usually think of our closest friends hanging on a cross. Usually we want to help our friends get down from the cross. We want our friends to be happy, to enjoy life. Yet, there is no doubt that sacrifice is part of friendship. Jesus said, "No one has a greater love than this, to lay down one's life for one's friends" (John 15:13). If friendship was simply looking for one happy day after another without sharing sorrow, it would not be real friendship but a type of narcissism or self-love. To love another for the sake of the other is to love like God. Only one who has known or experienced compassionate love can share this love with another. In her letters to Agnes, Clare asks Agnes to become a friend of Christ by learning to love like Christ. Seeing the love of God poured out in the crucified Spouse, Agnes is to grow in the same spirit of self-giving love.

For the Franciscans, to love God is to love a crucified God, a God of reckless, scandalous love. It is difficult to love a God of reckless love without becoming somewhat reckless in love oneself. Loving this type of God requires a public display of affection. Bonaventure states that as we ascend to God, that is, as we move inwardly into deeper relationship with God (since to "ascend" is to go "inward") we are to become ever more crucified to the world, that is, willing to suffer out of love for the sake of the other. At first the thorns and bristles of trying to live deep, compassionate love are difficult because all too often we want to go the way of individualism, privatism and selfishness. We desire God but the path is harsh, so the world is crucified to us because we find everything in the world difficult as we try to find (and love) God—our neighbors, our friends and families. However, as we persevere in prayer and deepen our trust in God, as we become more open to grace and rely more on God's mercy then the path of self-giving love becomes easier. We become crucified to the world. Learning to love by way of self-gift and becoming a friend of Christ goes hand-in-hand with a growth in self-knowledge, knowledge of God and the freedom to surrender. When prayer brings us to this level of relationship with God, then we are crucified for the sake of the world since one chooses to die for all in order to please God.[10] Thus, to ascend to union with God is to enter into the mystery of God as love, especially as this mystery of love is expressed in the crucified humanity of Christ. The more deeply we enter into friendship with Christ, the more we reflect this friendship by a willingness to love our neighbor. There is a short Jewish tale that captures the essence of this relationship to God. "A young woman once said to an old woman, 'what is life's heaviest burden'? And the old woman said, 'to have nothing to carry.'"[11] The type of love that gives life and brings one to the fullness of life is love for another, the type of love that ultimately is the gift of oneself. This love is most clearly expressed in those who are friends of God.

The centrality of the Crucified in the life of Francis suggests that Francis became a friend of Christ because he sought to follow Jesus who lived out of depth of love in obedience to the Father. The obedience of love led Jesus to the prophetic margins of announcing the kingdom despite opposition, misunderstanding and rejection. Christ left us an example, Francis said, that we might follow in his footprints.[12] In his *Earlier Rule* Francis claims that "our friends are all those who unjustly inflict upon us distress and anguish, shame and injury, sorrow and punishment, martyrdom and death. We must love them greatly for we shall possess eternal life because of what they bring to us."[13] One could readily conclude that either Francis had a lot of friends (because he had a lot of enemies) or he had very few friends because his idea of friendship was rather peculiar. Francis' thought in this passage seems contradictory to the human spirit. We usually do not count as friends those who harm or injure us. But he reflects here the gospel message of Christian love: "Love your enemies, do good to those who abuse you, bless those who curse you, pray for those who abuse you.... If you love those who love you, what credit is that to you? For even sinners love those who love them" (Luke 6:27–33). And here is the key to friendship with God. We are asked to love in a transcending manner, to go beyond our natural inclinations, to extend ourselves in love because God lives in the enemy and in the one who injures us. The one who loves God by loving the enemy is a friend of Christ. Although Francis the saint seems to have attained this level of love in his life, we can be sure that this type of love did not come easy to Francis, the cloth merchant-turned-beggar, as the story of the leper suggests. His biographers tell us that, as a young man, Francis loathed the sight of lepers; however, touched by God's grace he experienced a change of heart and one day bent down to kiss the hand of a leper and to give alms. The kissing of the leper's hand marked a turning point in Francis' life. He began to do penance and to acquire the spirit of compassionate love, and somehow a space opened up within him to embrace those he would otherwise reject. We might say that he came to embrace the leper by learning to embrace the leper within himself. Only when he came to a clearer knowledge of himself, his own weakness and smallness, could he see the greatness of God in the leper and those shunned by society.

While the story of the leper symbolizes friendship with God for Francis, the image that best symbolizes friendship is that of the good shepherd. This is one of the images that Francis used in his writings that he adopted from the Gospel of John. In John 10 the author speaks of the Good Shepherd as one who knows his sheep and who lays down his life for his sheep freely out of love (v. 14–18). This idea is supported in John 15:13 where the author writes, "no one has greater love than this, to lay down one's life for one's friends." The crucified Christ is the Good Shepherd, the one who laid down his life for his sheep. Francis was attracted to the image of the Good Shepherd because it spoke to him of the loving relationship between the Father and the Son. To love the Father in Francis' view is to become like the Son, crucified in love. Francis warned against a superficial understanding of the good shepherd or merely recalling the deeds of the saints who followed the good shepherd. "It is a great shame for us," he wrote, "that while the saints actually did these things [imitate the Good Shepherd], we wish to receive glory and honor by merely recounting their deeds" (*Admonition* 6.3). Francis was a man of action and he desired that his followers live in the spirit of Christ's crucified love in a world torn apart by violence, greed and domination. In his *Admonition Six* he provides a concrete description of what it means to follow Christ, the Good Shepherd. In his view, those who wish to glorify God must be willing to sacrifice their lives:

> Let all of us, brothers, look to the good shepherd who suf-
> fered the passion of the cross to save his sheep. The sheep
> of the Lord followed him in tribulation and persecution, in
> insult and hunger, in infirmity and temptation, and in every-
> thing else, and they have received everlasting life from the
> Lord because of these things. Therefore, it is a great shame
> for us, servants of God, that while the saints actually did
> such things, we wish to receive glory and honor by merely
> recounting their deeds.[14]

There is no doubt that, for Francis, the image of the Good Shepherd reflects the great love of God for us in Jesus Christ. He sees that through the sacrifice of the Shepherd we are brought into union with the Father, an idea that is highlighted in chapter twenty-two of his *Earlier Rule*:

> Let us have recourse to him as *to the shepherd and guardian of our
> souls*, who says: "I am the good shepherd who feeds my
> sheep and I lay down my life for my sheep." *All of you are
> brothers. And do not call anyone on earth your father, for one is Your
> Father, the One in heaven. And do not let yourselves be called teachers*

for your teacher is the One Who is in heaven. Let us, therefore, hold onto the words, the life, and the teaching and the Holy Gospel of him who humbled himself to ask his Father for us and to make his name known to us, saying: *Father, glorify Your name and glorify Your Son so that Your Son may glorify You. I do not ask you to take them out of the world, but that you keep them from the evil one. I ask not only for them but also for those who will believe in me through them, that they may be brought to perfection as one, and the world may know that you have sent me and love them as you loved me.* (John 17:17–23)[15]

This passage clearly shows the influence of John's Gospel on Francis' thought. Although the idea of martyrdom might seem quite radical to us, he believed that one who follows the Good Shepherd must be willing to lay down his or her life as Christ did out of love for God. One who has the spirit of martyrdom is a true friend of God. Even if one is not led to actual martyrdom, having the spirit of martyrdom, in Francis' view, joins one to Christ as spouse and brother. In his *Later Admonition and Exhortation,* he indicates that to be a spouse is to be joined to Christ in such an intimate way (*coniungitur*) that one's whole life becomes an imitation of Christ insofar as one has the spirit of Christ. This union with Christ, in a spirit of sacrificial love, is the fruit of prayer. Union with God for Francis is not some type of angelic state that exempts one from the difficulties of life. Quite the opposite. Union with God is to be like the Son, wholly attentive to the will of the Father out of love and obedience. Christ's love impelled him to voluntarily choose death by submitting to the will of the Father. In this way did Christ glorify the Father. If we sum up these ideas in light of Francis' life and writings we could say that to be in union with the Father means to follow the way of the cross. To love in the spirit of martyrdom is the path to happiness and eternal life.

In his *Major Legend* Bonaventure indicates that Francis had a great desire for martyrdom, following the example of Christ. He writes, "Set on fire by that perfect charity which drives out fear, he desired to offer to the Lord his own life as a living sacrifice in the flames of martyrdom so that he might repay Christ, who died for us, and inspire others to divine love."[16] This desire for martyrdom impelled Francis to go to Egypt around 1219 to preach the gospel to the Muslims. Bonaventure tells us that Francis and his brother companion were savagely seized, "cruelly and contemptuously" dragged away, treated with insults, beaten and put in chains.[17] However, Francis eventually made his way to the Sultan to preach the gospel. Standing before the Sultan, he announced the Good News of Jesus Christ by his example of peace and love. Francis proclaimed what he lived—that he was a Christian (*Ego sum Christianus*).[18] According to Bonaventure, the Sultan overflowed with admiration for Francis and offered him gifts that he could use for the Christian poor or for the churches. Although the Sultan did not convert to Christianity, both he and Francis found common ground as brothers. In a broad sense, Francis and the Sultan became friends because they were willing to transcend their own boundaries so as to enter into the life of the other out of respect and mutual love. This episode of Francis' life reflects his spirituality of friendship as it is centered in the cross. Spiritual friendship means to be conformed to Christ and to love as he loved even if it means self-sacrifice. The bond of love not only conforms one to Christ but leads one into union with the Father; indeed, the Father is revealed in and through the one who is a friend of Christ. For Francis, apostolic activity does not arise *from* the contemplation of God; rather, it *is* the contemplation of God because the same Spirit of love that goes out to unite with our neighbors or our brothers and sisters is the same Spirit of love that joins us to God and enables us to see the truth of God in the reality of our world. Francis' desire to encounter the Sultan to preach the gospel was the same desire to be wholly united to God, like the Son, in obedience to the loving will of the Father. To see, to love and to become what we love reflects a deep level of friendship with Christ, as we find in Francis.

For Clare of Assisi too, friendship with Christ entailed a friendship of self-giving love. Whereas Francis emphasized martyrdom (symbolized by the Good Shepherd), Clare emphasized personal transformation in union with the crucified Spouse. Unlike Francis, Clare's letters reflect a more personal relationship with the poor Crucified. She directs Agnes to foster a deep friendship with Christ who will lead her to the fullness of her identity in God. In her first letter Clare writes, "be strengthened...out of an ardent desire for the Poor Crucified who for our sake took...the Passion of the Cross...and *so reconciled us to God the Father.*"[19] Clare calls Agnes not to a life of suffering but to a life of love; however, the path will take her through suffering following the footprints of the crucified spouse. Agnes is to embrace this God of overflowing love who comes to her in fragile flesh. She writes, "as a poor Virgin, embrace the poor Christ."[20] This Spouse, Clare continues, was "struck," "scourged" and was the "lowest among humans." Gaze on this mystery, consider it, contemplate it, so that you may come to imitate it.[21] Clare sees the assurance of this path in the mirror of the cross of San Damiano. She gazed at this mirror for almost forty years of her life and described the parameters of the mirror as poverty, humility and charity.[22] Poverty is the border of the cross. Here we see the Incarnation and consider the poor manger in which Jesus was born and the swaddling clothes he was wrapped in. Humility is the surface of the cross by which we consider Jesus' life, his untold labors and burdens. Finally, charity is the depth of the cross, the center, where the love of the Spouse is made visible. This is the mirror of the invisible God and the mirror of our image, "that mirror suspended on the wood of the Cross."[23] To follow Christ, Clare indicates, is to see his footprints of poverty, humility and charity in the mirror of the cross.[24] She was certain that if Agnes gazes on this mirror daily she would be transformed into the one she loves.

Clare was convinced that loving the crucified God would lead Agnes to happiness, joy and a share in the eternal banquet. After all, friendship means sharing in the gifts of the one who is friend and Clare was not shy about her ambition for eternal happiness. However, like Francis, she saw that such happiness could only be attained in union with the crucified Spouse. Her thought follows a coincidence of opposites. "If you suffer with him, you will reign with him; if you weep with him you shall rejoice with him; if you die with him on the cross of tribulation, you shall possess heavenly mansions."[25] Clare's thought reflects the essence of the Christian message: finite things pass away, only the eternal promises life. Therefore, the mystery of all human strivings—life and happiness—are gained through suffering and death. To become a friend of Christ is to discover this secret path of life even though it is a path that contradicts our natural inclinations and human sensibilities. Friendship with Christ assures us that if we enter this strange and sorrowful path of the cross we will arrive at the peace and happiness of heaven. It is not a path that we frequently hear about because it contradicts all the ideals of popular culture. Western culture not only defies death as part of life but it offers a superficial notion of friendship. Any friend who becomes a burden is probably worth a one-way ticket to a far away place. We certainly do not believe that we should suffer for our friends no less give up our lives for them. Yet, in Clare's view, friendship with God (which cannot be separated from friendship with one another) demands that the cross be at the center of relationship, for this is the path that brings us life. Only one who knows Christ can assume this path of friendship which includes suffering out of love for another and perhaps death, living in hope that beyond death the fullness of life prevails.

Friendship with Christ for both Francis and Clare shows itself in action. A love based on the poverty and humility of love must be put into practice in daily life and in deeds.[26] In his writings Francis provides many ways to live in crucified love. For example, he tells his followers that they are to rejoice in the good fortunes of others as well as their own[27]; they are to love brothers and sisters even when they are sick and cannot repay them[28]; they are to love the brothers and sisters who have sinned[29]; and to love their enemies, which is the summit of love.[30] For Francis, to love one's enemies is the sign of the Spirit's "holy manner of working" within us which is the fruit of prayer.[31] He claims that we truly love our enemies when we are not upset by the injury they inflict on us but are disturbed only by the evil which their sin inflicts on themselves.[32] Clare too lived in this spirit of crucified love. At the process of her canonization many of the witnesses spoke of Clare's self-giving love to her sisters, how she washed the mattresses of the sick sisters, how she washed and kissed the feet of the domestic sisters and how she defended the monastery against the invading Saracens by holding up a monstrance containing the Eucharist.[33] One of the sisters testified that "before she was sick, she [Clare] desired to go to those parts of Morocco where it was said the brothers had suffered martyrdom," indicating that Clare's spirit was very close to that of Francis.[34]

What Clare and Francis saw in the mystery of the crucified Christ was not a violation of human dreams and hopes but the God of self-giving love. It was this God who grasped their lives. They were convinced that suffering out of love for another, following the example of the Crucified Christ, leads to happiness, unity and peace because this is the path of friendship with God. Their notion of friendship was not based on needs and wants but on the desire for mutuality, fulfillment and happiness that they believed could only be found in God. And they discovered this path of friendship in something we usually reject—the cross. They understood that friendship is a mutuality of desires: God's desire for us and our desire for God. That is why the cross is the sign of friendship because here is the visible sign of God's unconditional love for us or, we might say, the pledge of God's friendship with us. But if we really desire friendship with God we must ask, what kind of God do we desire to be friends with? If somehow we find our answer apart from the cross, we will always be seeking the ideals of joy and happiness in the wrong places. Francis and Clare assure us that the happiness of friendship with God is found in the strange relationship of suffering and love. If we are willing to love by way of suffering we will be on our way to friendship with God. Yes, friendship with God may be strange but then again this is no ordinary God. Rather this is a God who is reckless in love, and the one who desires friendship with God must become reckless in love as well—loving unto death. People who are reckless usually wind up in trouble because they do crazy things. Imagine being reckless for the kingdom of God. Just think what might happen. Friends of God loving one another around the earth. Heaven breaking open in our midst. We have the power to make this happen.

Meditation

Take time today to consider your relationship with God and to honestly ask if you are on the path to friendship with God. Consider how you have been a friend of God and how you have experienced the friendship of God. The following prayer of Bonaventure may help you in your meditation:

> O my God, good Jesus, Although I am in every way with-
> out merit and unworthy, Grant to me, Who did not merit to
> be present at these events in the body, that I may ponder
> them faithfully in my mind and experience toward you, My
> God crucified and put to death for me, that feeling of com-
> passion which your innocent mother and the penitent
> Magdalene experienced at the very hour of your passion.
> (*The Tree of Life*)

The deepening of friendship with God is the path to union with God. The following questions may help you reflect on this path.

1. Pray and reflect on the passage, there is "no greater love than this, to lay down one's life for one's friends" (John 15:13). Do you see your-self as a friend of Christ? What are you willing to do to be a friend of Christ?
2. How is Christ's friendship a support for you?
3. What kind of role does the Holy Spirit play in your friendship with God?

NOTES

[1] Cousins, *Bonaventure*, 59, n.1.

[2] Clare of Assisi, 3 *LAg* 12 (*Écrits*, 103). Engl. trans. Armstrong, *Clare of Assisi: Early Documents*, 45. For a more detailed examination of Clare and mirror spirituality see Regis J. Armstrong, "Clare of Assisi: The Mirror Mystic," *Cord* 37.5 (1985): 195–202.

[3] Clare of Assisi, 3 *LAg* 15 (*Écrits*, 104). Engl. trans. Armstrong, *Clare of Assisi: Early Documents*, 46. See also Francis of Assisi, "A Letter to the Entire Order" (29) where he writes, "Hold back nothing of yourselves for yourselves. That He who gives Himself totally to you may receive you totally!" Engl. trans. *FA:ED* I, 118 (*Écrits*, 250).

[4] Clare of Assisi, 3 *LAg* 24 (*Écrits*, 106). Engl. trans. Armstrong, *Clare of Assisi: Early Documents*, 46.

[5] Bonaventure, "Sermon on the Feast of the Transferal, 1267," 738. Engl. trans. *FA:ED* II, 738.

[6] Ibid.

[7] Francis of Assisi, "A Letter to the Entire Order" 39 (*Écrits*, 252). For the meaning of these terms, see Octavian Schmucki, "St. Francis' Level of Education," *Greyfriars Review* 10 (1996): 153–71. According to Dominic Monti ("Francis as Vernacular Theologian," 21, n. 3) the translation of this phrase in *Francis and Clare: The Complete Works*, ed. Regis J. Armstrong and I. Brady (New York: Paulist, 1982), 59 is more accurate than that in *FA:ED* I, 119.

[8] Bonaventure, "Sermon on the Feast of the Transferal." Engl. trans. *FA:ED* II, 743.

[9] Bonaventure, "Instructions for Novices," 2.7 in *The Writings of the Order*, vol. 5, *Works of Saint Bonaventure*, trans. Dominic Monti (New York: The Franciscan Institute, 1996), 155.

[10] In his *Triplici via* ("Triple Way or Love Enkindled," in *The Works of Bonaventure*, vol. 1, *Mystical Opuscula*, trans. José de Vinck [Paterson, NJ: St. Anthony Guild Press, 1960]) Bonaventure describes the ascent toward perfect love: "In the first, the world is crucified to man; in the second, man is crucified to the world; in the third, man is crucified for the sake of the world, since one chooses to die for all in order that all may please God." Engl. trans. De Vinck, *Triple Way*, 76. This scheme of spiritual perfection can be likened to the classical stages of purgation, illumination and union with God.

[11] Mary Jo Leddy, *Reweaving Religious Life: Beyond the Liberal Model* (Mystic, CT: Twenty-Third Publications, 1990), 46.

[12] Francis of Assisi, *Later Admonition and Exhortation* 13 (*Écrits*, 230). Engl. trans. *FA:ED* I, 46.

[13] Francis of Assisi, *Earlier Rule* 22.1 (*Écrits*, 162). Engl. trans. *FA:ED* I, 79.

[14] Francis of Assisi, *Admonition VI* (*Écrits*, 100). Engl. trans. *FA:ED* I, 131.

[15] Francis of Assisi, *Earlier Rule* 22.32–55 (*Écrits*, 166–168). Engl. trans. *FA:ED* I, 80–1.

[16] Bonaventure, *Leg.maj* 9.5 (*EM*, 77). Engl. trans. *FA:ED* II, 600.

[17] Bonaventure, *Leg. maj* 9.8 (*EM*, 80). Engl. trans. *FA:ED* II, 602.

[18] See Francis de Beers, *We Saw Brother Francis*, trans. Maggi Despot and Paul Lachance (Chicago, IL: Franciscan Herald Press, 1983), 96; J. Hoerberichts, *Francis and Islam* (Quincy, IL: Franciscan Press, 1997), 3–6.

[19] Clare of Assisi, 1 *LAg* 13-14 (*Écrits*, 86). Engl. trans. Armstrong, *Clare of Assisi: Early Documents*, 36.

[20] Clare of Assisi, 2 *LAg* 18 (*Écrits*, 96). Engl. trans. Armstrong, *Clare of Assisi: Early Documents*, 42.

[21] Clare of Assisi, 2 *LAg* 20 (*Écrits*, 96). Clare writes, "Your Spouse, though more beautiful than the children of men became, for your salvation, the lowest of men, was despised, struck, scourged untold times throughout his entire body, and then died amid the suffering of the cross." Engl. trans. Armstrong, *Clare of Assisi: Early Documents*, 42.

[22] Clare of Assisi, 4 *LAg* 19–23 (*Écrits*, 114). Clare writes, "Look at the border of this mirror, that is, the poverty of him who was placed in a manger and wrapped in swaddling clothes.... Then, at the surface of the mirror, consider the holy humility, the blessed poverty,

the untold labors and burdens that he endured for the redemption of the whole human race. Then in the depth of this same mirror, contemplate the ineffable charity that led him to suffer on the wood of the cross and to die there the most shameful kind of death." Engl. trans. Armstrong, *Clare of Assisi: Early Documents*, 50–1.

[23] Clare of Assisi, 4 *LAg* 24 (*Écrits*, 114). Engl. trans. Armstrong, *Clare of Assisi: Early Documents*, 51.

[24] In her second letter (2 *LAg* 7) Clare writes, "Instead, as someone zealous for the holiest poverty, in a spirit of great humility and the most ardent charity you have held fast to the footprints of him to whom you have merited to be joined as a Spouse." Engl. trans. Armstrong, *Clare of Assisi: Early Documents*, 40.

[25] Clare of Assisi, 2 *LAg* 21–22 (*Écrits*, 98). Engl. trans. Armstrong, *Clare of Assisi: Early Documents*, 42.

[26] Francis of Assisi, *Earlier Rule* 11.6 (*Écrits*, 144). Engl. trans. *FA:ED* I, 72.

[27] Francis of Assisi, "A Prayer Inspired by the Our Father" 5 (*Écrits*, 278); *Admonition* 17.1 (*Écrits*, 108).

[28] Francis of Assisi, *Admonition* 24 (*Écrits*, 112).

[29] Francis of Assisi, "A Letter to the Ministers" 9-11 (*Écrits*, 262).

[30] Francis of Assisi, *Earlier Rule*, 22.1 (*Écrits*, 162); *Later Rule* 10.10 (*Écrits*, 196); *Admonition* 9 (*Écrits*, 102); "Prayer Inspired by the Our Father" 8 (*Écrits*, 278).

[31] Francis of Assisi, *Later Rule* 10.8 (*Écrits*, 196).

[32] Francis of Assisi, *Admonition* 9 (*Écrits*, 102). Engl. trans. *FA:ED* I, 132.

[33] See "The Acts of the Process of Canonization," Third Witness, Seventh Witness; "The Versified Legend of the Virgin Clare," in *Clare of Assisi: Early Documents*, 150, 162, 208–09.

[34] "The Acts of the Process of Canonization," Sixth Witness in *Clare of Assisi: Early Documents*, 159. The author writes, "She also said Lady Clare had such a fervent spirit she willingly wanted to endure martyrdom for love of the Lord. She showed this when after she had heard certain brothers had been martyred in Morocco, she said she wanted to go there."

Chapter Six

THE HEART TURNED TOWARD GOD

Believing, hoping and loving
With my whole heart, with my whole mind
And with my whole strength,
May I be carried to you, beloved Jesus,
As to the goal of all things,
Because you alone are sufficient,
You alone are good and pleasing
To those who seek you and love your name.
For you, my good Jesus,
Are the redeemer of the lost,
The savior of the redeemed,
The hope of exiles,
The strength of laborers,
The sweet solace of anguished spirits,
The crown and dignity of the triumphant,
The unique reward and joy of all the citizens of heaven,
The renowned offspring of the supreme God
And the sublime fruit of the virginal womb,
The abundant fountain of all graces,
Of whose fullness we have all received.

—Bonaventure
The Tree of Life

There is a mail order firm by the name of "Heart Matters" that sends me catalogs every month hoping that it can inspire my heart or that of someone else through note cards, CDs and "Precious Moments" figurines. Sometimes I think we clutter our hearts with a lot of stuff that we think "matters" but in the end it is simply a lot of stuff. What matters to the heart is more than things (although "things" may, indeed, inspire it at times). The heart thrives on the life-giving spirit of love. Friendship is a matter of the heart. It is the heart's desire to share life with another person. The heart (*cor*) is the center of the whole personal life of the human person. It is the seat of intellectual and spiritual life, of reason and will, and the inner movements of experiencing life (or the lack of it).[1] The heart is the place of encounter, where God reveals himself to us. As Jesus tells us in the Gospel, "where your treasure is, there will your heart will be also" (Luke 12:34). Francis believed that the heart was the seat of the will, the root of sin and the place of conversion. The heart is made for God and is the proper dwelling place of the most blessed Trinity; it is the place of encounter between person and Creator. In the heart the person receives the life-giving awareness of God; it is where one comes to know God. The human heart is created to be the home of the Spirit of the Lord through whose life-giving power relationship with God becomes reality. To surrender the "heart" is the fundamental act of following Christ.

Francis understood that contemplation begins with a pure heart. Contemplation is not some type of intellectual union of the mind with God but, as we have already said, it is a deep penetrating vision of reality. That is why all those who seek God must, at some point in their lives, contemplate God. Those who strive for purity of heart never cease to adore God, and to see God and his work. When the heart is enlightened by knowledge, it encounters God by seeing the dimension of mystery present in everything, whose absolute center is God alone. Turning one's heart toward God implies a great variety of attitudes. It means not only fixing one's gaze upon the mystery of God (which is central for Francis) but a series of steps: holding fast to his word, loving, serving, adoring God, acting according to the Spirit, living in humility and patience and loving one's neighbor, and even one's enemy.[2] As Francis indicated in his *Admonitions*, the heart must not turn away from God under "pretexts" of occupations.[3] Too often today in our busy world we hear complaints of "I do not have enough time" to pray, or "I am too busy to pray." We are burdened by appointments, commitments, responsibilities or simply overloaded with the demands of daily life, journeying through life in the fast lane of a complex culture. When we arrive at "burnout" and wonder why life is so empty, we may recall Francis' admonition that our hearts may turn from God under the disguise of being "too busy."

In his *Earlier Rule* Francis suggests that the heart is the dwelling place of the Spirit, that is, of an energy or force that influences the activities or movements of the human person. In this respect, it is the place where the Spirit of the Lord struggles with the spirit of the flesh:

> Let us be very much on our guard that, under the guise of some reward or assistance, we do not lose or take our mind away from God. But, in the holy love which is God, I beg all my brothers, both the ministers and the others, after overcoming every impediment and putting aside every care and anxiety, to serve, love, honor and adore the Lord God with a clean heart and a pure mind in whatever way they are best able to do so, for that is what he wants above all else.[4]

Francis calls us to real discernment. Prayer means centering one's life in God by "putting aside every care and anxiety," that is, surrendering one's heart to God, and striving for purity in love. The source or origin of prayer for Francis is the Spirit who rests in the faithful making them the "home and dwelling" of the Trinity.[5] The Spirit, the true Adorer of the Father, produces in those in whom the Spirit resides an inclination to reach out to God, a movement of "holy prayer and devotion."[6] The Spirit urges those in whom the Spirit dwells to pray with a pure heart and with all the diversity and richness that such prayer implies.

The first holy activity of the Spirit of Lord, according to Francis, is to pray always with a pure heart. In the *Earlier Rule* he exhorts all the brothers to serve, love and adore the Lord God with a clean heart and a pure mind, for he desires this above all things: "And let us adore him with a pure heart, because it is necessary to pray always and not lose heart; for the Father seeks such people who adore him."[7] The same theme is found in the *Later Admonition and Exhortation* where he uses the expression "spirit of truth" to suggest that it is the Spirit of the Lord who produces in us the act of praying with a pure heart. In two places he associates this spirit of prayer with the Our Father,[8] indicating that for him the prayer with a pure heart and in the spirit of truth is the Our Father. This is the first prayer, Celano states, that Francis taught the brothers.[9] The Our Father is a spirit-filled prayer. The Son and Spirit direct the worship and love of the praying person to the Father. Entering into the heart of the mystery of God means being drawn by the Spirit into that communion of life and love between Jesus and the Father.

For Francis, only God is truly pure. The person who desires friendship with God must strive to be free from all attachments and from all commitments that are exclusively human or in relation to earthly realities. This does not mean that we are to give up our friends or sacrifice our desire for a better job or position. Rather, we may understand attachment here as possessiveness. We are called to be dispossessed of earthly things so as to possess God. To possess means to "cling to," to hold on to something so tightly that other possibilities are "squeezed out." Each of us is called to be poor, to empty ourselves of all that we cling to so that we may receive the gift of the Holy Spirit. For Francis, the way to purity of heart is by following Christ, especially his powerlessness and service to all and his total dependence on his heavenly Father. Following Christ means "living in obedience [to the will of the Father], without anything of one's own and in chastity."[10] Purity of heart is not simply detachment or self-emptying. Rather it is a total surrender to its only true and most perfect good—union with the Trinity in and through the power of the indwelling Spirit. Francis believed that the pure of heart always adore and see the Lord God living and true. In his *Admonition* 16 he claimed, "Blessed are the pure of heart for they shall see

God. The truly pure of heart are those who despise the things of earth and seek the things of heaven, and who never cease to adore and behold the Lord God living and true with a pure heart and soul."[11] What does this mean? It means that our hearts are pure when we view earthly things from "on high," that is, when we see their true value. We "seek the things of heaven" when we search for the mystery of God present in everything, when we realize that the whole creation reflects the goodness of God. Since the Spirit of the Lord lives in a pure heart, those who strive for purity of heart are true temples of the Spirit, offering prayer unceasingly to the Father.

To turn the heart toward God, to make a place within the heart for the Spirit of truth to dwell, is to be joined to the Word and, in turn, to the Father. A life of turning one's heart to God is a deepening of life in the Trinity. The door to the Trinity opens with the Spirit. In his *Earlier Rule* Francis uses the Gospel passage of the seed (Luke 8:11) to indicate that only the pure of heart have the proper soil to receive the Word of God which is the spirit of truth and which brings forth spirit and life (John 6:64). We need, therefore, to check our hearts and ask, are we prepared to receive the Word of life or do our hearts have rocky soil in which the Word can easily get crushed? Francis reminds us that we are dwellings and houses for the Word of God, and he encourages us to develop a prayer that is continual, attentive and enriched by loving relationships. Our prayer must be vigilant, that is, alert to the movements of our heart. Prayer that leads to the indwelling Word requires a certain level of interiority, an inner dialogue with God. Francis challenges us to look carefully at the soil of our hearts so that the seed of the Word might grow and be fruitful.[12] In Francis' view, to provide a dwelling place for the Word of God is to bear its fruit in one's life.

Francis placed a great emphasis on the Word of God as a living Word, the Word of life. This is the Word that took flesh in Jesus, the Word that comes to us in the Scriptures and in the sacraments, especially the Eucharist, and the Word that fulfills our lives when it dwells in our hearts. As a life-giving Word, Francis made every effort to ensure that the Word became his life, and he called his followers to do the same. To live in the Word of God as a life-giving Word is to allow the

Spirit of gospel truth to shine through in everything we do, that is, we are called to give birth to Christ. Francis writes,

> We are spouses when the faithful soul is united by the Holy
> Spirit to our Lord Jesus Christ. We are brothers, moreover,
> when we do the will of his Father who is in heaven; moth-
> ers when we carry him in our heart and body through love
> and a pure and sincere conscience; and give him birth
> through a holy activity, which must shine before others by
> example.[13]

Through the Spirit, we are to take on the Word in our own lives so that we become the Word. How? By coming to a true knowledge of who we are and coming to a deeper understanding of who we are meant to be. God utters each of us as a little "word" so that, from all eternity, each of us is meant to express something of God. Because we often live with divided selves—where the spirit longs for God but the flesh longs for something else—we fail to live in the truth of our identity, and thus we fail to be the "word" that God intended us to be. Prayer of the heart, that unceasing prayer where God breathes in us and our hearts are turned toward God, allows us to deepen our identity in God. And in that deepening of life in God by which we become more of our true selves, the Word shines forth in our lives. We become an expression of the Word of God. Thus, when we allow the Word to take root within us through prayer and the indwelling of the Spirit then we bring the Word to life. In Francis' view, nothing is to hinder us from this vocation nor should we desire anything else: "Let us desire nothing else, let us want nothing else, let nothing else please us and cause us delight except our Creator, Redeemer and Savior, the only true God, let nothing hinder us, nothing separate us, nothing come between us."[14] That is, let us focus our energies on God alone.

Life in God should be a daring adventure of love—a continuous journey of putting aside our securities to enter more profoundly into the uncharted depths of God. Too often, however, we settle for mediocrity. We follow the rules and practices of prayer but we are unwilling or, for various reasons, unable to give ourselves totally to God. To settle on the plain of mediocrity is really to settle for something less than

God that leaves the heart restless and unfulfilled. A story from the desert fathers reminds us that giving oneself wholly to God can make a difference:

> Abba Lot went to see Abba Joseph and said to him, "Abba, as far as I can I say my little office, I fast a little, I pray and meditate, I live in peace and as far as I can, I purify my thoughts. What else can I do?" Then the old man stood up and stretched his hands towards heaven. His fingers became like ten lamps of fire and he said to him, "If you will, you can become all flame."[15]

To be turned into fire. Why do we not desire to become "all flame"? Well, there are various reasons, the first of which is fire is dangerous. It is destructive; it burns and it destroys. Fire is consuming; it devours whatever is in its path. But fire is also light and warmth. Fire can melt and transform things. Jesus said, "I came to bring fire to the earth and how I wish it were already kindled!" (Luke 12:49). The universe story began in a fiery explosion. Jesus initiated a new fire, the fire of the Holy Spirit sent as tongues of flames upon the disciples at Pentecost. Christians are called to be the fire of God's transforming love. We are to harness the energies of love so that we may help all of creation move toward its completion in God. What prevents us from this call? What keeps us settled on the plain of mediocrity?

Francis, Clare and Bonaventure identify the source of complacency in the human heart. Happiness, peace, love and justice are ultimately matters of the heart because the heart is the "hearth" of the human person, the place where the kindling of the Spirit can take place. Bonaventure claimed that we cannot be made happy unless we rise above ourselves "not by an ascent of body but of the heart."[16] Prayer, in Bonaventure's view, begins in the heart: "When you pray, gather up your whole self, enter with your Beloved into the chamber of your heart and there remain alone with Him, forgetting all exterior concerns, and so rise aloft with all your love and all your mind, your affection, desire and devotion, enter into the place of the wonderful tabernacle, even to the house of God."[17] For Bonaventure, the heart is the place of knowledge and rest, as well as the place of love. It is the place where one enters into solitude and fosters the desire for God. "Be sure always to guard your heart well," he writes.[18] The heart is the "holy of holies," the place of sacrifice and self-offering, the place where the Spirit of God dwells, the Spirit that joins us to Christ and to the Father. The first act of divine worship takes place in the heart because it is here that God dwells with us and where God shares with us the sufferings and joys of our lives. In a letter to a Poor Clare nun, Bonaventure wrote, "Your heart is to be an altar of God. It is here that the fire of intense love must burn always. You are to feed it every day with the wood of the cross of Christ and the commemoration of his passion."[19] In Bonaventure's view, the heart makes every person a member of the royal priesthood. Every person is to offer sacrifice to God through the lifting up of one's heart to God.

If the heart is the place of worship, it is also the place of intimacy with God. The fire of love in the human heart is to be enkindled not only by our desire for God but by our willingness to offer God every aspect of our lives, that is, every aspect of our humanity, including the struggles, pains, hurts and rejections of our lives. Nothing about our lives is too distant from God. No corner of our lives is foreign to God. Rather, God has entered into the darkness of every human heart and has loved us in the midst of pain and rejection. This is the meaning of the cross and its significance for our relationship with God. As Bonaventure tells us:

> Let your love lead your steps to Jesus wounded, to Jesus crowned with thorns, to Jesus fastened upon the gibbet of the cross. Not only see in His hands the print of the nails, not only put finger into the place of the nails, not only put your hand into His side, but enter with your whole being through the door of His side into Jesus' heart itself. There transformed into Christ by your burning love for the Crucified, pierced by the nails of the fear of God, wounded by the spear of superabounding love, transfixed by the sword of intimate compassion, seek nothing, desire nothing, wish for no consolation, other than to be able to die with Christ on the cross. Then you may cry out, "With

Christ, I am nailed to the cross. It is now no longer I that
live, but Christ lives in me."[20]

Who awakes in the morning wishing for nothing other than to die with
Christ on the cross? In a culture that essentially denies death, no one
desires to die unless one has fallen into despair. How do we interpret
this spirituality as a life-giving one? Clare reminds us that the Christian
God is a crucified God. Any other type of God is one of our own projections and desires, an idolatrous God who we create in our own
image. In his search to find the deeper meaning of God in a world of
violence and suffering, the contemporary theologian Jürgen Moltmann
pondered the mystery of the cross as the mystery of God. He wrote,

> When the crucified Jesus is called the 'image of the invisible
> God,' the meaning is that this is God, and God is like this.
> God is not greater than he is in this humiliation. God is not
> more glorious than he is in this self-surrender. God is not
> more powerful than he is in this helplessness. God is not
> more divine than he is in this humanity. The nucleus of
> everything that Christian theology says about 'God' is to be
> found in this Christ event.[21]

This too is Bonaventure's thought. Everything that can be said about
God is expressed in the visible figure of Jesus on the cross. "He withstood all these sufferings in order to set you aflame with love for him;
in order to move you, in return, to love him with all your heart, all your
soul and all your mind."[22] Thus, if we are to find God, and ourselves in
God, we must search the depths of our own hearts and find within these
depths the mystery of Christ crucified, because in these depths is the
God who loves us.

Clare of Assisi, like Bonaventure, had a clear focus on the crucified
Christ as the spouse of transforming love. Only in union with this
spouse, she professed, can we really become transformed in the love of
God and radiate the beauty of God's image in our lives. In her second
letter to Agnes, Clare described the crucified Spouse as "more beautiful
than the children of men [who] became for your salvation, the lowest
of men, despised, struck, scourged untold times throughout his entire

body, and then died amid the suffering of the cross."[23] It is amazing that Clare shows optimism in gazing on this crucified Spouse. She indicates a real assurance to Agnes that following this path of the Crucified will lead her to the victory of love: "If you suffer with him, you will reign with him. If you weep with him, you shall rejoice with him; if you die with him on the cross of tribulation, you shall possess heavenly mansions in the splendor of the saints and, in the book of life, your name shall be called glorious among people."[24] What Clare highlights is the Christian message—death leads to life. Love, by way of suffering, leads to the fullness of love. If we accept Clare and Bonaventure's spiritual path, then we must admit that it takes a spirit of poverty and humility to penetrate the mystery of the Christian God. Too often, we look for God in all the wrong places. We expect to find a God of power and might but instead we encounter a God of crucified love. To know this God we must let go of our fears, expectations and speculations of what God is like and freely enter the mystery of the cross. We can enter this mystery by entering into our own hearts, the mystery of our own humanity with its joys and sorrows, gifts and wounds. Here is where God dwells, in the midst of our fragile humanity, the God who bends low to embrace us in love.

Perhaps the greatest obstacle to meeting God on the cross is the obstinacy of the human heart. "O human heart," Bonaventure writes, "you are harder than any hardness of rock…you are not struck with terror nor moved with compassion."[25] The heart that cannot feel, cannot love. How is it, Bonaventure decries, that we can look at Jesus on the cross and not be moved to tears? "How is it that we have such cold hearts that we are not prepared to endure anything for our Lord's sake?"[26] Our hearts neither burn nor glow with love. "Our love for God has turned to frost and ice within us," Bonaventure writes to the Poor Clares. "Most certainly, if we were burning with love, we would shed our worldly garments to follow the naked Christ. Those who feel very hot take off their clothes. It is a sign of great coldness in us that we should snatch so eagerly at these perishable things."[27]

Maybe our hearts are too tightly bound within us. Maybe the vessels of our hearts are blocked by fear, self-centeredness, anger, hurt, rejection. Whatever it is that prevents the fire of the heart from burning, Bonaventure asks us to look at the cross and to see how God has loved us by descending into the depths of human suffering. The Seraphic Doctor arouses the sluggishness of the human heart by vividly describing the sufferings Jesus endured:

> Thrown roughly upon the wood of the cross, spread out, pulled forward and stretched back and forth like a hide, he was pierced by pointed nails, fixed to the cross by his sacred hands and feet and most roughly torn with wounds he was stripped of his garments, so that he seemed to be a leper from the bruises and cuts in his flesh from the blows of the scourges.[28]

This is the God who loves us, Bonaventure indicates, the God who was crucified for us. As he writes: "[May] I ponder in my mind and experience toward you, my God crucified and put to death for me, that feeling of compassion."[29] This is the God whom we are to embrace, the God who kisses us: "Behold the head of Christ leaning down to kiss us, His arms stretched out for an embrace, His hands pierced for a gift of blood, His side opened for loving, His whole body extended for a complete spending of Himself."[30] Bonaventure adds a caveat to those who reject this God of love made visible in the crucified Christ: "Woe to those who crucify again for themselves the Son of God, adding to the pain of Him they have wounded."[31] What a strong warning to those who claim to be Christian! How often do we stop to ask ourselves, do we crucify God? Are we adding to the pain of the One who is already wounded? And who is this crucified God? This God is the crucified God of abused children, the crucified God of the victims of war, the crucified God of battered wives and husbands, the crucified God of the elderly and the mentally disabled, the crucified God of the crucified earth and all the crucified people in the world.

As Christians we are asked to be transformed in love so that the wounds of God may be healed by love. We are asked to take down Christ from the cross and hold him in our hearts, to become this Christ of self-giving love so that dying with Christ [in love] we may rise with

Christ to new life. We are called to an intimate relationship with the crucified God, to participate in the Christ mystery. This is a difficult call and oftentimes we are weighed down by our own immediate concerns or disappointments. Or sometimes we just prefer mediocrity. Bonaventure wrote,

> If at times, things are sad, burdensome, tiring or bitter run
> without delay to Jesus on the cross. Look at his crown of
> thorns, his iron nails and the spear in His side; contemplate
> the wounds of the hands and feet, the wounds of the head
> and side, the wounds of the whole body; remember who it
> was that suffered so bitterly and bore such outrage for you,
> and how He must have loved you.[32]

The freedom of God is such that God respects our mediocrity without trying to force us to realize our capacity for complete transformation. Yet, the invitation to total love is always present, as Bonaventure writes,

> Do you long to be transformed into him to the point where
> your heart is aflame with love? Just as iron when heated to
> the point where it becomes molten can take the imprint of
> any mark or sign, so a heart burning fervently with love of
> Christ crucified can receive the imprint of the Crucified
> Lord himself or his cross. Such a loving heart is carried over
> to the Crucified Lord or transformed into him. That is what
> happened with Saint Francis.[33]

Do we long to be transformed into God and what are we willing to offer? Do we prefer hearts of smoke (smoldering fires) or do we want hearts of fire? The author of Timothy writes, "For this reason I remind you to rekindle the gift of God that is within you through the laying on of my hands; for God did not give us a spirit of cowardice, but rather a spirit of power and of love and of self-discipline" (2 Timothy 1:6–7). The exemplary lives of Francis and Clare indicate that the price of love is high; it is the price of one's life. Neither of them settled for a timid spirit. They understood that love cannot be bought nor is it an intellectual exercise. Love requires the totality of being and being-in-love demands the fullness of life. Thus we are asked to turn our hearts to the Lord: to fix one's gaze upon the mystery of God and hold fast to his word—loving, serving, adoring God—acting according to the Spirit, living in humility and patience and loving one's neighbor and even one's enemy. The heart must not be turned away from God under pretexts of occupations. We are called to turn our hearts to the Lord at all times and seasons, in every country and place, every day and all day.[34] Only in this way can the heart see the total reality of God and creation in God. But this totality of the heart turned to God is a death of the self-centered ego. Bonaventure writes,

> Whoever loves this death can see God because it is true beyond doubt that man will not see me and live. Let us then die and enter into the darkness; let us impose silence upon our cares, our desires and our imaginings. With Christ crucified let us pass out of this world to the Father....You are the God of my heart, and the God that is my portion forever.[35]

Only when we are willing to die with Christ on the cross, to offer up our possessions, our sufferings, our self-centeredness, everything that we cling to in our lives, everything that prevents us from real relationship with God—only when we can nail these things to the cross in exchange for love can we say, "God is the rock of my heart and my portion forever."

This passing over into God through the Crucified Christ is dangerous because a heart centered in God is free, free to spread fire upon the earth, free to love, free to bear witness to the dangerous memory of Jesus. What does a heart centered in God do? A heart centered in God is subversive. A heart centered in God can be threatened with death and not fear because it knows that God is its portion and rock. Jesus before Pilate shows us what a heart centered in God is like. Pilate asked, "Do you not know that I have the power to release you, and the power to crucify?" (John 19:10). "You would have no power over me," Jesus answered him, "unless it had been given to you from above" (John 19:11). Modern saints, too, show us that a heart centered in God is free to speak the truth and to act in the name of truth. The prophetic words of the Salvadoran Bishop Oscar Romero during his last homily reflect the heart of one who had found freedom in God:

> You have just heard in Christ's gospel that one must not love oneself so much as to avoid getting involved in the risks of life that history demands of us, and that those who try to fend off the danger will lose their lives, while those who out of love for Christ give themselves to the service of others will live, like the grain of wheat that dies, but only apparently. If it did not die, it would remain alone. The harvest comes about only because it dies, allowing itself to be sacrificed in the earth and destroyed. Only by undoing itself does it produce the harvest.... This holy mass, now, this Eucharist, is just such an act of faith.... May this body immolated and this blood sacrificed for humans nourish us also, so that we may give our body and our blood to suffering and to pain—like Christ, not for self, but to bring about justice and peace for our people.[36]

The heart centered in God loves without counting the cost; it loves like Jesus. God comes to us to set our hearts free, to enkindle in us the fire of love. What prevents us from accepting this gift given so freely? Why do we settle for ashes when we are called to be fire? According to Francis, Clare and Bonaventure, the answer is given in the mystery of the crucified Christ. For this crucified Christ is God and God is like this; God is not greater than in his humiliation; God is not more powerful than in his passion. So we must ask, who is the God to whom we are praying? Who is the God of my heart?

Meditation
Take some time today to sit quietly in a place of solitude. Try to free yourself from distractions and enter into your heart. Spend some time dwelling in the center of your heart by meditating on the following words of Bonaventure:

Your heart is the altar of God. It is here that the fire of
intense love must burn always. ("On the Perfection of Life")

As you pray to the God who dwells within your heart, consider the following questions:

1. Where is the center of your heart, in "God" or in "yourself"?
2. What prevents you from accepting the gift of God's "kenotic" love?
3. Do you want to be transformed in God's love? What are you willing
   to risk? To change?
4. Pray the text of 2 Timothy 1:6–7: "For this reason I remind you to
   rekindle the gift of God that is within you through the laying on of
   my hands; for God did not give us a spirit of cowardice, but rather a
   spirit of power and of love and of self-discipline." What prevents you
   from becoming fire?

NOTES

[1] Thaddée Matura states that "the human heart plays a prominent role in Francis' thought,
for he regarded it as the unifying center of the person, the true self, so that, when it is per-
verted and turned away from God, it becomes a poisoned well-spring that corrupts everything." See Thaddée Matura, *Francis of Assisi: The Message in His Writings*, trans. Paul Barrett (New
York: The Franciscan Institute, 1997), 100.

[2] See Thaddée Matura, "The Heart Turned Towards the Lord," *Cord* 44 (1994): 11.

[3] Matura, "Heart Turned Towards the Lord," 11. See also *Admonitions* IX, XI, XV (*Écrits*, 102,
106).

[4] Francis of Assisi, *Earlier Rule* 22.25–31 (*Écrits*, 166). Engl. trans. *FA:ED* I, 80.

[5] Francis uses a string of Scriptures related to the significance of the Spirit and the
indwelling Trinity. For example in his *Earlier Rule* 22.27 (*Écrits*, 166) he writes: "Let us always
make home and a dwelling place there for him who is the Lord God Almighty, Father, Son
and Holy Spirit....And let us adore him with a pure heart....God is Spirit and those who
adore him must adore him in Spirit and truth." See *FA:ED* I, 80.

[6] Francis writes in his *Later Rule* 5.2 (*Écrits*, 188) "do not extinguish the Spirit of holy prayer
and devotion to which all temporal things must contribute." See *FA:ED* I, 102.

[7] Francis of Assisi, *Earlier Rule* 22.29-30 (*Écrits*, 166). Engl. trans. *FA:ED* I, 80.

[8] Francis of Assisi, *Earlier Rule* 22.28 (*Écrits*, 166); *Later Admonition and Exhortation*, 21.

[9] Thomas of Celano, "The Life of Saint Francis," *FA:ED* I, 222.

[10] Francis of Assisi, *Earlier Rule*, 1.1 (*Écrits*, 122). Engl. trans. *FA:ED* I, 63.

[11] Francis of Assisi, *Admonition* XVI (*Écrits*, 106). Engl. trans. *FA:ED* I, 134.

[12] Armstrong, *St. Francis of Assisi*, 96.

[13] Francis of Assisi, *Later Admonition and Exhortation*, 51–53 (*Écrits*, 236). Engl. trans. *FA:ED* I, 49.

[14] Francis of Assisi, *Earlier Rule*, 23.9–10 (*Écrits*, 176). Engl. trans. *FA:ED* I, 85.

[15] *Sayings of the Desert Fathers: The Alphabetical Collection*, Joseph of Panephysis 7, trans. Benedicta Ward (London: Mowbray, 1975), 88.

[16] Bonaventure, *Itin.* 1.1 (V, 296). Engl. trans. Cousins, *Bonaventure*, 59.

[17] Bonaventure, *Perf. Vit.* 5.5 (VIII, 119). Engl. trans. De Vinck, "On Perfection of Life" 236. The biblical idea of the heart as the spiritual center of the human person was a common theme throughout the Middle Ages. Bonaventure uses the word in the traditional fashion whereby the heart is the seat of intelligence and love, with a special emphasis on the affective aspect. See Jean Châtillon, "Cor et cordis affectus," in *Dictionnaire de Spiritualité*, vol. 2 (Paris), 2289–2300. See especially column 2298 for Bonaventure's use of the term.

[18] Bonaventure, *Perf. Vit.* 1.2 (VIII, 108). Engl. trans. De Vinck, "On Perfection of Life," 212.

[19] Bonaventure, *Perf. Vit.* 6.1 (VIII, 120). Engl. trans. De Vinck, "On Perfection of Life," 239.

[20] Bonaventure, *Perf. Vit.* 6.1 (VIII, 120). Engl. trans. De Vinck, "On Perfection of Life," 239–40.

[21] Jürgen Moltmann, *The Crucified God: The Cross of Christ as the Foundation and Criticism of Christian Theology*, trans. Margaret Kohl (New York: HarperCollins, 1991), 205.

[22] Bonaventure, *Perf. Vit.*, 6.9 (VIII, 123). Engl. trans. De Vinck, "On Perfection of Life," 245.

[23] Clare of Assisi, 2 *LAg* 20 (*Écrits*, 96).

[24] Clare of Assisi, 2 *LAg* 21-22 (*Écrits*, 98). Engl. trans. Armstrong, *Clare of Assisi: Early Documents*, 42.

[25] Bonaventure, *Lignum vitae* (*Lig. Vit.*) 29 (VIII, 78). Engl. trans. *The Tree of Life* in Cousins, *Bonaventure*, 154. In his section on the passion in his *Tree of Life*, Bonaventure repeatedly emphasizes the hardness of the human heart.

[26] Bonaventure, "The Evening Sermon on Saint Francis, 1262." Engl. trans. *FA:ED* II, 726.

[27] Bonaventure, *Perf. Vit.* 3.8 (VIII, 114). Engl. trans. De Vinck, "On Perfection of Life," 225.

[28] Bonaventure, *Lig. Vit.* 26 (VIII, 78). Engl. trans. Cousins, *Bonaventure*, 149.

[29] Bonaventure, *Lig. Vit.* 32 (VIII, 80). Engl. trans. Cousins, *Bonaventure*, 158.

[30] Bonaventure, *Perf. Vit.* 6.10 (VIII, 123). Engl. trans. De Vinck, "On Perfection of Life," 245.

[31] Ibid.

[32] Bonaventure, *Perf. Vit.* 6.11 (VIII,123). Engl. trans. De Vinck, "On Perfection of Life," 246.

[33] Bonaventure, "Evening Sermon on Saint Francis." Engl. trans. *FA:ED* II, 727.

[34] Matura, "The Heart Turned Towards the Lord," *Cord* 12.

[35] Bonaventure, *Itin.* 7.6 (V, 311). Engl. trans. Cousins, *Bonaventure*, 116.

[36] Archbishop Oscar Romero, *Voice of the Voiceless: The Four Pastoral Letters and Other Statements* (Maryknoll, NY: Orbis, 1996), 193.

Chapter Seven

CONTEMPLATION: SEEING AND LOVING

Aroused by everything to divine love,
He rejoiced in all the works of the Lord's hands
And through their delightful display
He rose into their life-giving reason and cause.
In beautiful things he contuited Beauty itself
And through the footprints impressed in things
He followed his Beloved everywhere,
Out of them all making for himself a ladder
Through which he could climb up to lay hold of him
Who is utterly desirable.

—Bonaventure
The Major Legend of Saint Francis

A student once wrote in a paper, "I never thought I could strive for contemplation. I thought contemplation is for special people, not for the ordinary person like me." My response to him was, "no person is too ordinary to contemplate God. It is essential to living the Christian life." The idea that everyone is called to contemplation was entirely new for this student and I am sure for many others as well. We don't view the Christian life as one of contemplation and we certainly don't speak of Christian life as a contemplative life or hear it preached this way on Sunday. Yet, if we have been following the path of Franciscan prayer all along, we realize that this path of prayer is a contemplative one. The progression of prayer that leads to contemplation begins with the gaze on the crucified Christ and continues to penetrate the depths of this reality until the one who gazes comes to see the heart of charity hidden in the heart of Christ. We have already described contemplation as a penetrating vision but we must also concede that it is a deepening of love, a continuous action of ongoing transformation, since nothing is more liberating and active than love. This love not only enables one to see more clearly and deeply into the depths of the Spouse, the heart of Christ, but to feel and taste the hidden sweetness of God.[1]

In his first *Admonition*, Francis describes contemplation as seeing God in Christ with the eyes of the Spirit. He describes contemplation as the vision of God's humility. The Father who dwells in "inaccessible light," he writes, is humbly present in the Son through the love of the Spirit. This is the meaning of Incarnation which we encounter in the Eucharist, God's humbling movement toward humanity: "Each day he humbles himself as when he came from the royal throne into the Virgin's womb; each day he himself comes to us, appearing humbly."[2] Contemplation for Francis and Clare is a penetrating gaze that gets to the heart of reality.[3] It is looking into the depths of things and seeing them in their true relation to God. Bonaventure calls this type of penetrating vision "contuition" whereby one sees concrete reality in itself and in God.[4]

For Clare, contemplation begins with the mirror of the crucified Christ. That is why she advised Agnes to see herself in the mirror each day. It is Clare, I believe, who provides a common path to contemplation because what she advocates is daily prayer before the cross—something every person can do. To accept God in the Crucified is to accept God in our own lives and this means to accept who we are. Clare draws a relationship between contemplation and self-identity. The more we contemplate or dwell on the mystery of Christ by gazing upon the Crucified, the more we discover our own identity. We might say that the cross provides the most honest reflection of ourselves. When we gaze on this mirror of the cross we not only see who God is, self-giving love, but gazing on this God of humble love leads us to reflect on our own lives. So the gaze is self-reflective. The crucified Christ, who is the image of God, is the image in which we are created and thus the basis of our identity.[5] If we gaze long enough, that is, if gazing becomes a way of life then it will lead to a new level of self-knowledge. We will come to a new understanding of ourselves and this understanding will be creative, since it will transform the one who gazes in the mirror of the cross into a reflection of the image itself. That is, the more we contemplate Christ by gazing upon the cross, the more we will come to resemble Christ. This image of God, revealed in the one who gazes on the mirror of the Crucified, will be expressed as a new "birth" of Christ in the believer. To place oneself in the mirror of the cross, therefore, is to expose oneself to the joys and sorrows of being human, the joy of God's all-embracing love and the sorrow of the Spouse "despised, struck, and scourged."[6] By dwelling in the mirror of the cross—heart, mind and soul—we are called to "transform our whole being into the image of the Godhead itself."[7] In this way, we are called to a life of contemplation.

Clare had particular insight with regard to the capacity of the human person to image God. In her fourth letter to Agnes, she draws a relationship between contemplation and the human face. She tells Agnes to "gaze upon that mirror each day...and continually *study your face* within it, so that you may adorn yourself *within and without* with beautiful robes."[8] Although Clare does not define the goal of contemplation explicitly, she describes this goal broadly as conversion through imitation of Christ and interior transformation in order to reflect the face of Christ to the world. She is certain that such transformation can only take place in the mirror of the cross. She speaks of the human face as the sign of transformation because the face discloses the person in a particular way and therefore reflects one's personal identity or self-expression.[9] The face symbolizes the person because it both reveals what a person is and yet conceals the inner depth of the person. The idea of the "face" not only connotes uniqueness and distinction, that which makes a person who she or he is, but it connotes form or expression since it is the face that one sees. To study one's face in the cross means to question the form or shape of one's life. The face is the epiphany of God. Only by becoming truly human, like the beloved spouse, does one disclose the face of God.

If contemplation is to study one's face in the mirror of the cross, then contemplation is the way the self achieves its true form as image of God. To study one's face in the cross is to ask, what am I? What distinguishes me? For Clare, we cannot really answer these questions without looking at our image in the mirror of the cross. The self is not a substance separate from God, according to Clare, but is created precisely in relationship to God. To come to the knowledge of who we are is to discover the treasure within each of us, the image of God in which we are created and by which we are in relationship with God.[10]

Because identity is the creation of the self as image of God, it is recognizing that my full self lies in God; thus I must find God within myself if I am to enjoy the fullness of my humanity. In Clare's words, it is finding "the incomparable treasure hidden in the field and in the heart of the human."[11] Prayer that leads to contemplation of the crucified Spouse leads to an ongoing creation of self whereby the emergence of who we are in the mirror of the Crucified is expressed in what we become (our "face") and in the virtues we acquire inwardly and outwardly. As we come to be who we are called to be in relation to God (self-identity), God shows himself to the universe through his constant and continual creation of ourselves. The self that comes to be through a union with God in love is the self in which God is reflected, that is, the image of God. The enfleshment of God in one's life through contemplation is the basis of transformation, and transformation is the renewal of Christ in the world.

Although the cross is central in Clare's spirituality, hers is not a spirituality of sin and guilt, rather it is one of freedom and transformation. The cross is the mirror of truth, where we come to see ourselves in our capacity to love and in our brokenness. An honest acceptance of who we are with our strengths and weaknesses is liberating in Clare's view. Dwelling in the mirror of the crucified Christ is to lead to that place of inner freedom, a freedom that is born of the joy of the Spirit[12] and of union with the Spouse.[13] When Clare tells Agnes to "study her face in the mirror each day" she is urging her to become transformed in union with the one she loves. For Clare, to be transformed is to "put on Christ" or to "re-present Christ"; transformation *is* imitation insofar as Christ "comes alive" in one's life. When we cling to the crucified Spouse with all our heart and open up to the embrace of the Crucified, then we welcome the Spirit of God into our hearts, allowing that Spirit to transform us in love. Thus, a continuous gaze on the crucified Spouse ultimately leads to imitation.[14]

Clare's way of prayer is a spiral that goes to the depth of the human person's capacity for God and the infinite love of God for the human person. Her understanding of contemplation complements that of Francis who described contemplation as "seeing with the eyes of the Spirit."[15] For Francis, one must have the Spirit of the Lord (who joins one to Christ)[16] to see into the depths of things.[17] This too is Clare's idea. One who is joined to Christ has the spirit of Christ and imitates Christ through the very expression of one's face. It is the Spirit that conforms one to Christ and enables one to see into the depths of things. The gift of the Spirit is the fruit of poverty by which one is free enough to accept the embrace of God's love in the embrace of the crucified Christ. What is original to Clare is that transformation/imitation of Christ cannot take place apart from contemplation, and contemplation involves self-identity or acceptance of oneself in relation to God. As one comes to a deeper truth of oneself in relation to God, so too, one is filled with the Spirit of God. It is the Spirit that allows one to see with the heart and to contemplate the other by a penetrating gaze. In light of this relationship Clare writes, "Therefore that mirror suspended on the wood of the cross, urged those who passed by to consider, saying: 'All you who pass by the way, look and see if there is any suffering like my suffering!'" (Lam 1:12)[18] It is difficult to see another person's suffering if we have not come to terms with our own suffering. We cannot see clearly the truth of the other if we have not first seen clearly the truth of ourselves (although we do much better seeing other peoples' faults rather than our own!) A life of poverty that invites the Spirit into our lives can lead to the humble place of self-acceptance, where we see ourselves for what we really are. When the spiritual eyes of the heart are open to self-knowledge then they can see into the depths of the other, our neighbors who are our sisters and brothers. Seeing into the depths of others means seeing others for what they truly are, images of God. If we really could see the light of God in others rather than their defects, then we could love others more deeply. We could love others not simply to satisfy our own needs but we could love others for themselves and share in their sufferings. Clare indicates in her writings that as one sees the sufferings of Christ in the other, so one is to love. As she says to Agnes, "From this moment, then, O Queen of our heavenly King, let yourself be inflamed more strongly with the fervor of charity!"[19] What Clare suggests is that contemplation is not a preliminary step to transformation/imitation but rather one must strive to be transformed in Christ in order to contemplate the truth (depths) of Christ. We cannot really see the depths of God's goodness in others unless somehow we see God's goodness within ourselves and, if we can do this, then we are on the way to transformation. The mutual relationship between contemplation and transformation governed by self-identity involves self-acceptance and self-awareness or, we might say, accepting the poverty of our human condition. Contemplation deepens, as we continue to be transformed in Christ, by coming to the truth of our identity.

While Clare draws a connection between contemplation, self-knowledge and identity, Bonaventure describes contemplation as the union of knowledge and love, that is, the attainment of wisdom.

Contemplation, according to Bonaventure, is integral to the journey to God because it was the condition and privilege of humanity before the fall. Initially, humans stood upright in the garden of paradise and were able to contemplate the light of divine wisdom reflected in the mirror of creation.[20] Throughout creation, creatures could discern the reflection of the Creator. Being made in the image of God humans were oriented toward God through the gift of grace. The very nature of the human person, in Bonaventure's view, is to contemplate God because we are, by nature, oriented toward God. However, because of sin humans became trapped in darkness and ignorance, causing them to lose the way to contemplate God. Bonaventure writes, "As a result the human, blinded and bent over, sits in darkness and does not see the light of heaven unless grace with justice come to his aid against concupiscence and unless knowledge with wisdom come to aid against ignorance. All this is done through Jesus Christ."[21] Prayer is essential to restoring our full humanity because prayer seeks the grace that will bring the soul to the point where it is reoriented completely toward God.[22] "Just as no one comes to wisdom except through grace," he writes, "so no one comes to contemplation except by penetrating meditation, a holy life and devout prayer."[23] For Bonaventure, continuous prayer, purity of heart and desire for union leads the seeker of God to the contemplation of God.

In his *Soul's Journey into God* Bonaventure maps out the journey to contemplation through a unique synthesis of mystical theology, medieval symbolism and the example of Francis of Assisi. He begins on the level of creation with its order and beauty. Because creation speaks to us of God but is a limited expression of God, gazing on creation causes us to search inward for God, which leads us to self-knowledge and knowledge of God. We are led to consider the image of God in which we are created and, for Bonaventure, this consideration draws us into the mystery of Christ. As we ponder the mystery of God in Christ and the image in which we are created, we are led into the depths of the Trinity, the infinite communion of self-diffusive love. This ascent "upward" into the Trinity of love is one ultimately of the heart. Knowledge is important because we cannot love what we do not know;

however, intellectual knowledge can lead us only to the doorstep of the Trinity. It is love that leads us into the heart of the Trinity and, for Bonaventure, this love is the deepest knowledge of God.

Wisdom is knowledge deepened by love; it is an experiential knowledge of God. As the fullness of love, it is an interior affective "tasting" or delighting in the divine.[24] Wisdom is the vision of the heart whereby the heart sees the truth of things and thus knows in a way more deeply than the (intellectual) mind itself could ever grasp. It delights in God as good revealed in the interior of the soul. Wisdom is the gift of the Spirit given to one who has "passed over" into God; it is the fruit of union, which leads to a proper relationship with God and creation. One who has arrived at a deep relationship with God, in which God's grace predominates in one's life, arrives at wisdom because one's heart is no longer centered in "oneself" but in God. Although Bonaventure's doctrine of contemplation may seem speculative, it is really experiential. Because Christ is the wisdom of God, the type of union he describes that leads to contemplation is union with the crucified Christ. His theology is Pauline: the cross is the book in which the entire wisdom of Christ is written.[25] In this respect, his notion of contemplation complements the teaching of Clare. For Bonaventure and Clare, contemplation is the fruit of union with the crucified Christ. Bonaventure describes Francis' encounter with the Crucified on the mountain of La Verna as the encounter with the beauty of divine wisdom.[26] Outwardly the figure of the crucified seraph who Francis saw appeared disfigured and distorted but inwardly it was illuminated.[27] The Stigmata or the wounds of Christ that Francis received were proof that Christian wisdom was "ploughed into [Francis'] flesh" by the "finger of the living God."[28]

According to Bonaventure, Francis reached the heights of contemplation through poverty and humility. Contemplation entailed not only a full loving relationship with God in Christ but Francis was restored as a fully loving human person in union with Christ. In Bonaventure's view, Francis became a person of wisdom. He "ascended in Christ" by "descending" in poverty and humility through imitation of the crucified humanity of Christ, and this imitation of Christ led him to the heights of contemplation and glory. In his sermons Bonaventure claims that love drew Francis to the heights of contemplation. In particular, compassionate love forged Francis into the image of Christ. This love emerged from his continuous gaze on the beloved crucified Christ. "Ardent love is a quality of the heart," Bonaventure wrote,

> And the stronger this love burns in a person's heart, the more heroic and virtuous are his deeds.... Just as iron when heated to the point where it becomes molten can take the imprint of any mark or sign, so a heart burning fervently with love of Christ crucified can receive the imprint of the Crucified Lord himself or his cross. This is what happened with Saint Francis.[29]

The spirit of compassionate love grew in Francis through a life of unceasing prayer and of seeing his unworthiness before the overflowing compassionate and merciful love of God. Bonaventure wrote that "he was always at prayer, and he wept so much that he lost his sight."[30] According to Celano "his heart's love showed in the wounds of his body...he wept "loudly over the passion of Christ, as if it were constantly before his eyes."[31]

Contemplation is the fruit of union in love; it is the vision of the lover who gazes on the beloved. The biographers of Francis tell us that after he encountered the God of compassionate love in the visible figure of the crucified Christ, Francis' "vision" began to change. Prayer that leads to an openness of the Spirit and the indwelling of the Word and Father leads to an experience of penetrating vision by which one sees God in concrete reality. The Spirit, welcomed in the silence of prayer, transforms the vision of our hearts to see the invisible presence of God hidden in the depths of ordinary reality. As Francis "ascended" the mountain of love in union with Christ, he began to see the world around him differently—the leper became his brother and the poor and sick were visible expressions of God's overflowing love. What was initially "bitter" for Francis became "sweet" as he contemplated the goodness of God in fragile humanity.

In Bonaventure's view, love bound Francis to the things of creation and opened his eyes to the truth of God in creation. He came to realize that the Incarnation sanctifies all creation. In Jesus not only does the fullness of divinity reside, but in him is subsumed all of creation as well. Earth, water, fire and air, the four cosmic elements, are not just God's creation; they are made holy by Jesus Christ, in whom the elements of the universe are further sanctified.[32] As Francis' heart opened to the overflowing goodness of God, he began to "see" God's goodness incarnate—Christ—in every aspect of creation. Everything spoke to Francis of the infinite love of God. Trees, worms, flowers by the side of the road—all were for him saints gazing up into the face of God. Creation became the place to find God and, in finding God, Francis realized his intimate relationship to all of creation. Bonaventure describes Francis as a "contuitive person" who made all of creation a ladder by which he could climb up and embrace the beloved. He wrote, "In beautiful things he contuited Beauty itself and through the footprints impressed in things he followed his Beloved everywhere, out of them all making for himself a ladder through which he could climb up to lay hold of him who is utterly desirable."[33] Francis saw God reflected on every level of creation, from stars to sun and moon to tiny earthworms and lambs, to his brother friars and brother lepers. He discovered that the world is the cloister of God because each individual created thing bore a unique relationship with God and reflected the power, wisdom and goodness of God. He came to realize that creation is a theophany, a manifestation of God, or, as the poet Gerard Manley Hopkins wrote, the world is charged with the grandeur of God. Everything bows down before the divine, like the stars in Joseph's dream.[34]

Francis lived in love and, by loving other creatures, let them be, encouraging them to grow in their uniqueness, sharing with them their very being. Bonaventure claims that Francis was moved with a sense of relatedness (piety) to all things and that he spared nothing at all, neither mantles nor tunics nor books...all these he gave to the poor.[35] He discovered that his life was incomplete without relationship to even the tiniest creatures of creation. Bonaventure writes that "he [Francis] would call creatures, no matter how small, by the name of brother or sister because he knew they shared with him the same beginning."[36] Everything in creation spoke to Francis of God. Just as he was impressed by the compassionate love of God in his encounter with the Crucified, so too he came to see that same love impressed on every level of creation. He found himself in a familial relationship with creation calling out to "brother lamb,"[37] "sister birds,"[38] and "sister cricket."[39] In Bonaventure's view, Francis' depth-seeing was not merely a passive seeing but a deep penetrating gaze into the truth of the other, opening up his heart to receive the other in an embrace. In this way, the overflowing goodness of God permeating all of creation, first made visible in the beloved Christ, became visible in the disfigured flesh of the leper and the tiny things of creation.

In his *Canticle of Creatures* Francis praised God through the elements of the universe, reminding us that we humans are as dependent on the elements of creation as they are dependent on us. With his marvelous respect for creatures of all kinds, for sun, moon, stars, water, wind, fire and earth, Francis came to see that all creation gives praise to God. The sun by being itself praises God and the stars glittering in the sky praise God because each star radiates the goodness of God. We might say that Francis came to appreciate the whole cosmos as the astonishing image of God.[40] The *Canticle* signifies that the whole creation is a cosmic Incarnation—earth, air, water, sun, moon, stars—all are related to Brother Sun who is the splendor and radiance of the Most High. We might read Francis' *Canticle* as foreshadowing the new creation, when we will find ourselves related to all things in the spirit of reconciliation and peace. It brings to our awareness that the entire creation is charged with the goodness of God so that, even in eternal life, creation will offer praise and glory to the Most High.

While it was Christ who enabled Francis to see the truth of reality, namely, that everything is imbued with the goodness of God, it is how Francis lived in Christ that shaped his relationship to creation. Penance, poverty, humility and compassion were the values that forged Francis into a "cosmic brother," one who was related to all creatures and to the elements of creation. Through penance he recognized his sinfulness and need for conversion. Through poverty he became aware of the human tendency to possess, as he realized his radical dependency on all things. Through humility he realized his solidarity with all creatures. Through compassion he came to feel for the things of the earth, including the tiniest of creatures. Creation became a ladder by which he could ascend to God, not by transcending creation but by embracing it as brother. For by embracing the good things of creation, Francis came to embrace the whole Christ who is the Word of the Father. On the level of creation, therefore, as on the level of humanity, Francis realized his relationship to other creatures because of his intimate relationship to Christ. Encountering Christ as the sacrament of God's love enabled him to contemplate God's love in every aspect of creation. The relationship between seeing and loving, which is evident in the writings of Francis and Clare, marks a type of contemplation that distinguishes Franciscan evangelical life.[41] Contemplation is not a solitary flight to God or an intellectual union. Christ goes away, Bonaventure said, when the mind tries to behold him with the intellect.[42] Rather, contemplation is a penetrating gaze of the other and of oneself—of the other, as the one in whom God is enfleshed, and of oneself, as one who is capable of union with God. Contemplation, therefore, is accepting the other, the God who comes to us in fragile humanity and in the fragile things of creation. It is finding the truth of who we are in relation to the incarnate Word of God and incarnating that Word in our own lives. One who "puts on Christ" in one's own life and sees the suffering of Christ in the other must ultimately love like Christ by way of compassionate love. Contemplation is seeing with the eyes of the heart. It is the vision of one who has found one's center of gravity in God. To enter into the love of contemplative union for Clare is to re-center one's heart in God. "Love him totally," she writes, "who gave himself totally for your love."[43] Bonaventure, too, described the journey into God as one of ecstatic love, a "re-centering" of one's heart in God. In his *Soul's Journey into God* he wrote: "Let us, then, die and enter into the darkness...with Christ crucified let us pass out of this world to the Father so that when the Father is shown to us, we may say with Philip: It is enough for us.... You are the God of my heart, and the God that is my portion forever."[44]

To see, to love and to become what we love is the fruit of contemplation that can only be realized when we accept the poverty of being human and, in this poverty, accepting the embrace of God's love for us which marks the greatness of the Christian vocation. Clare recognized the tremendous dignity of the human when she wrote,

> Indeed, is it not clear that the soul of the faithful person, the most worthy of all creatures because of the grace of God, is greater than heaven itself, since the heavens with the rest of creation cannot contain their Creator and only the faithful soul is His dwelling place and throne, and this only through the charity that the wicked lack.[45]

What Clare indicates here is that contemplation is bound to transformation. We cannot help seeing—gazing—on the crucified God for long without being changed. And this change, this gazing on the God of self-giving giving love, must eventually impel us to love by way of self-gift. In this way, we realize the greatness of our vocation that is to bear Christ, to become a Christic person. Only in and through this "Christification" do we see the world as the sacrament of God, and all of creation as holy ground. Engagement with the other becomes an engagement with God. Contemplation is not directed toward heaven but toward the fullness of the Incarnation. Clare reminds us that we are the Body of Christ and we are called to live in the mystery of Christ as co-workers of God: "I consider you a co-worker of God himself and a support of the weak members of his ineffable Body."[46] Just as God sees fragile humanity and binds himself to humanity, so too we are to see fragile humanity and bind ourselves to that fragile humanity. Because contemplation is grounded in concrete reality, the one who contemplates must ultimately act in a new way according to what one sees. Like Francis, one who gazes on the compassionate love of God is able to see the suffering of others and to feel with them in their struggles and, in this seeing and feeling, act according to the law of love.

To contemplate is to grow in love, not to become angelic but to grow in a depth of relationship of love. Contemplation is relational because in seeing the truth of God's goodness in the other, we see the truth of ourselves, our own goodness but also our weaknesses and failings. That is why the mirror of the cross is central to a real relationship with God. In the cross we see who we are and we strive to embrace our own identity, what makes each of us unique. Gazing on the Crucified should lead us to realize that God loves us *as we are* with our gifts and failings. When we can accept God's love in ourselves then we can gaze on the love of God in our neighbors, our brothers and sisters, the tiny creatures of creation, the sun, moon and stars and, yes, even our enemies. We can gaze on them with their strengths and weaknesses, beauty and ugliness, through which is reflected the overflowing goodness of God.

While this Franciscan path of contemplation is desperately needed in our world today as we face massive suffering and vast ecological crises, we still live, in our western culture, with an emphasis on rationality, order and mind. Because our "I" is separated from the world around us, we struggle to be incarnational people and to see our world imbued with divine goodness. We fail to contemplate God's love poured out into creation. In his *Soul's Journey into God* Bonaventure put forth sharp words for those who fail to see the overflowing goodness of God on every level of creation:

> Whoever, therefore, is not enlightened by such splendor of
> created things is blind;
> Whoever is not awakened by such outcries is deaf;
> Whoever does not praise God because of all these effects
> is dumb;
> Whoever does not discover the First Principle from such
> clear signs is a fool.
> Therefore, open your eyes, alert the ears of your spirit, open
> your lips and apply your heart so that in all creatures you
> may see, hear, praise, love and worship, glorify and honor
> your God lest the whole world rise against you.[47]

The Franciscan path to God calls us to gaze on the crucified Christ and to see there the humble love of God so that we may, like Francis, learn to see and love the presence of God's overflowing goodness hidden, and yet revealed, in the marvelous diversity of creation. The one who contemplates God knows the world to be charged with the grandeur of God. Contemplation leads to a solidarity with all creation whereby all sorrows are shared in a heart of compassionate love, all tears are gathered in a womb of mercy, all pain is healed by the balm of forgiveness. The contemplative sees the threads of God's overflowing love that binds together the whole of creation in a web of infinite love. We are called to see deeply that we may love greatly. And in that great love, rejoice in the overflowing goodness of God.

Meditation

Contemplation is a matter of vision. Take some time today to consider how you "see" yourself and the world around you. Consider whether or not you are attentive to what you see and if this attention to others leads you closer to God. The following passage of Bonaventure may help you ponder the path of contemplation:

> In beautiful things he contuited Beauty itself and through the footprints impressed in things he followed his beloved everywhere, out of them all making for himself a ladder through which he could climb up to lay hold of him who is utterly desirable. (*The Major Legend of Saint Francis*)

How does this passage speak to you? What does it call you to do? As you continue to strive for contemplation or if you desire to deepen your life of contemplation, consider the following:

1. How do you understand contemplation? Do you seek to contemplate God?
2. How does prayer lead you to the vision of contemplation? What prevents you from this vision?
3. How does your contemplation lead to action? To love of your family, spouse, sisters and brothers? How does it relate to the hope of peace and justice in the world?
4. Meditate on Colossians 1:15–17 and Romans 8:38–39.

NOTES

[1] Clare of Assisi, 3 *LAg* 14 (*Écrits*, 103). Clare writes, "So that you too may feel what his friends feel as they taste the hidden sweetness of God." Engl. trans. Armstrong, *Clare of Assisi: Early Documents*, 45.

[2] Francis of Assisi, *Admonition* 1.16–17 (*Écrits*, 92). Engl. trans. *FA:ED* I, 129; Michael W. Blastic, "Contemplation and Compassion," 162.

[3] Blastic describes this phenomenological type of contemplation as distinctive of both Francis and Clare's paths of contemplation. See Blastic, "Contemplation and Compassion," 165.

[4] For a definition of "contuition" see Delio, *Simply Bonaventure*, 199.

[5] See Delio, "Clare of Assisi: Beauty and Transformation," 75.

[6] Clare of Assisi, 2 *LAg* 20 (*Écrits*, 96). Clare writes: "Your Spouse...was despised, struck, scourged untold times throughout his entire body, and then died amidst the sufferings of the cross." Engl. trans. Armstrong, *Clare of Assisi: Early Documents*, 42.

[7] Clare of Assisi, 3 *LAg* 12-13 (*Écrits*, 102). "Pone mentem tuam in speculo aeternitatis, pone animan tuam in splendore gloriae, pone cor tuum in *figura* divinae substantiae et *transforma* te ipsam totam per contemplationem *in imagine* divinitatis ipsius."

[8] Clare of Assisi, "The Fourth Letter to Agnes of Prague" (4 *LAg*) 14–16 (*Écrits*, 112–114). Engl. trans. Armstrong, *Clare of Assisi: Early Documents*, 50. See Delio, "Clare of Assisi: Beauty and Transformation," 75.

[9] The postmodern philosopher Emmanuel Levinas claims that the face of the genuine other should release us from all desire for totality and open us to a true sense of the infinite because inscribed in the face of the other is the trace of a transcendence. One cannot grasp the other in knowledge, for the other is infinite and overflows in the totality of comprehension and of being. See Edith Wsychogrod, *Saints and Postmodernism: revisioning moral philosophy* (Chicago: University of Chicago Press, 1990), 148; Robyn Horner, *Rethinking God as Gift: Marion, Derrida and the Limits of Phenomenology* (New York: Fordham University Press, 2001), 64–6.

[10] Bonaventure also makes this point in his *Soul's Journey into God*. See Itin. chs. 3–4 (V, 303–308).

[11] Clare of Assisi, 3 *LAg* 7 (*Écrits*, 102). Clare writes, "I see that by humility, the virtue of faith, and the strong arms of poverty, you have taken hold of that incomparable treasure hidden in the field of the world and of the human heart." Engl. trans. Armstrong, *Clare of Assisi: Early Documents*, 45.

[12] Clare of Assisi, 4 *LAg* 4 (*Écrits*, 110).

[13] Clare of Assisi, 4 *LAg* 10 (*Écrits*, 112).

[14] This idea is what Clare describes in her second letter to Agnes, 2 *LAg* 20 (*Écrits*, 96).

[15] Francis of Assisi, *Admonition* 1.20 (*Écrits*, 92). Engl. trans. *FA:ED* 1.129.

[16] Again, Francis gave primacy to the Spirit of the Lord as the one who makes life in Christ

possible. In his Letter to the Faithful he writes, "We are spouses when the faithful soul is united by the Holy Spirit to our Lord Jesus Christ." See his *Later Admonition and Exhortation* 51 in *FA:ED* 1, 49 (*Écrits*, 236).

[17] The notion of penetrating vision is distinctive of Franciscan contemplation. Bonaventure used the term "contuition" to describe this penetrating vision which sees a thing in itself and in its relation to God. For a definition of contuition see Delio, *Simply Bonaventure*, 199.

[18] Clare of Assisi, 4 *LAg* 25 (*Écrits*, 114). Engl. trans. Armstrong, *Clare of Assisi: Early Documents*, 51.

[19] Clare of Assisi, 4 *LAg* 27 (*Écrits*, 116). Engl. trans. Armstrong, *Clare of Assisi: Early Documents*, 51.

[20] Bonaventure, II *Sent.* d. 23, a. 2, q. 3, concl. (II, 544b–545b). Bonaventure states that Adam was able to contemplate God without hindrance in the mirror of creation because the mirror was not yet obscured by the effects of sin.

[21] Bonaventure, *Itin.* 1.7 (297–298). Engl. trans. Cousins, *Bonaventure*, 62.

[22] Bonaventure, *Circum. Dom.* 1 (IX, 137a); *Comm. Lc* n. 15, c. 21–52 (VII, 389b–402a).

[23] Bonaventure, *Itin* 1.8 (V, 298). Engl. trans. Cousins, *Bonaventure*, 63.

[24] Bonaventure, III *Sent.* d. 35, a. 1, q. 1, concl. (III, 774b). Bonaventure puts forth a doctrine of the spiritual senses in his *Soul's Journey into God*.

[25] Bonaventure, *De S. Andrea Apost. Serm.* 1 (IX, 469a).

[26] For those unfamiliar with Francis' life, the event of the Stigmata is significant. In 1224, two years before his death, Francis went up to the mountain of La Verna to spend forty days in solitude and prayer. While he was there praying, there appeared to him a seraph in the form of a crucified man. According to his biographers, this vision of the crucified seraph/man marked the event of the Stigmata or mystical wounds of Francis. No one knows exactly what happened on the mountain, as there were no eyewitnesses. However, Francis descended from the mountain apparently marked with the wounds of Christ.

[27] Bonaventure, *Leg. maj.* 13.10 (*EM*, 114).

[28] Bonaventure, *Leg. maj.* 13.10, 5 (*EM*, 114, 109).

[29] Bonaventure, "Evening Sermon, 1262." Engl. trans. *FA:ED* II, 727.

[30] Bonaventure, "Sermon on the Feast of the Transferal." Engl. trans. *FA:ED* II, 744.

[31] Thomas of Celano, "The Remembrance of the Desire of a Soul," 6.11. Engl. trans. *FA:ED* II, 250.

[32] Ilia Delio, *A Franciscan View of Creation: Living in a Sacramental World*, edited by Elise Saggau, vol. 2. Heritage Series (New York: The Franciscan Institute, 2003), 12.

[33] Bonaventure, *Leg. maj.* 9.1 (*EM*, 74). Engl. trans. *FA:ED* II, 596.

[34] Hans Urs von Balthasar, *Studies in Theological Style: Clerical Styles*, trans. Andrew Louth, Francis McDonagh and Brian McNeil, vol. 2, *The Glory of the Lord. A Theological Aesthetics*, ed. Joseph Fessio (San Francisco: Ignatius Press, 1984), 267.

[35] In his *Legenda major* Bonaventure states that "true piety filled Francis' heart...[that] he was moved with piety to all things." See *Leg. maj.* 8.1 (*EM*, 64). Engl. trans. *FA:ED* II, 586. See also Bonaventure, *Leg. maj* 8.6 (*EM*, 68). Engl. trans. *FA:ED* II, 590.

[36] Bonaventure, *Leg. maj* 8.6 (*EM*, 68). Engl. trans. *FA:ED* II, 590.

[37] Bonaventure, *Leg. maj* 8.6 (*EM*, 68). Engl. trans. *FA:ED* II, 590.

[38] Bonaventure, *Leg. maj* 8.9 (*EM*, 71). Engl. trans. *FA:ED* II, 592.

[39] Bonaventure, *Leg. maj* 8.9 (*EM*, 71). Engl. trans. *FA:ED* II, 593.

[40] The notion of the cosmos as the astonishing image of God is attributed to the contemporary theologian, Elizabeth Johnson. See her article "The Cosmos: An Astonishing Image of God," *Origins* 19/13 (September 12, 1996): 206.

[41] Francis of Assisi, *Earlier Rule* 17.3 (*FA:ED* I, 75); *Admonition* I (*FA:ED* I, 129); "A Letter to the Entire Order" 28 (*FA:ED* I, 118).

[42] Bonaventure, *Hex.* 2.32 (V, 342).

[43] Clare of Assisi, 3 *LAg* 15 (*Écrits*, 104). Engl. trans. Armstrong, *Clare of Assisi: Early Documents*, 46.

[44] Bonaventure, *Itin* 7.6 (V, 312). Engl. trans. Cousins, *Bonaventure*, 116.

[45] Clare of Assisi, 3 *LAg* 21–22 (*Écrits*, 104). Engl. trans. Armstrong, *Clare of Assisi: Early Documents*, 46.

[46] Clare of Assisi, 3 *LAg* 8 (*Écrits*, 102). Engl. trans. Armstrong, *Clare of Assisi: Early Documents*, 45.

[47] Bonaventure, *Itin.* 1.15 (V, 299). Engl. trans. Cousins, *Bonaventure*, 67–68.

Chapter Eight:

IMITATION: BECOMING WHAT WE LOVE

After true love of Christ
Transformed the lover into His image,
When the forty days were over that he spent in solitude
As he had desired,
And the feast of St. Michael the Archangel
Had also arrived,
The angelic man Francis
Came down from the mountain,
Bearing with him
The likeness of the Crucified,
Depicted not on tablets of stone or on panels of wood
Carved by hand,
But engraved on parts of his flesh
By the finger of the living God.

—Bonaventure
The Major Legend of Saint Francis

One of the most popular works in the history of Christian spirituality is *The Imitation of Christ* by Thomas à Kempis. This book provides a set of directives that appeal to the imagination and senses on following Jesus in this life and gaining the merits of eternal life. More recently the WWJD ("what would Jesus do?") movement, a revival of the nineteenth-century Protestant movement, has gained popularity, as people strive to live the gospel life by following the example of Jesus Christ. While these imitations of Christ (*imitatio Christi*) paths may be helpful, the notion of imitation as described in the Franciscan path of prayer does not follow the logic of these other movements. The difference between the Franciscan *imitatio Christi* and the Thomas à Kempis/WWJD movements is that, in the latter, the Incarnation is extrinsic to the believer. When I ask, "what would Jesus do?" I am looking to the example of Jesus as a moral guide to make the right decision or perform the right action. Jesus leads and I follow.

The Franciscan path is different because it does not ask, "what would Jesus do?" but "how does Jesus live in me?" For the Franciscans, the Incarnation is intrinsic to human personhood. What we are about as humans and what we are to become as children of God is integrally related to the person of Jesus Christ. Christ is not merely a person we follow, as if following John or Jim, nor is salvation about the "dos and don'ts" of being saved. Rather Christ, the Word incarnate, is the person in whom each person finds his or her unique meaning and origin. The logic of the Franciscan *imitatio Christi* is God's self-emptying love which is incarnate in the person of Jesus Christ. To say that Jesus is the theophany or manifestation of God means that in the form of Jesus' life, God has been fully revealed. Jesus Christ is the image of God because Christ is the "Word" or the perfect self-expression of the Father. Therefore, it is Christ who is the perfect image of the invisible God (Colossians 1:15).[1]

The word "image" means a pressing outward of an inward content in all forms of "expression."[2] To imitate is to image. As image of God we are created in such a way as to imitate God. When the Word became flesh, the perfect image of God (the Father) was expressed in history and time. This means that everything we can know about God is revealed to us in the life of Christ. From his poor and humble birth to his prophetic life on the margins, the life of Christ expresses the Father's free decision to make himself visible to all.[3] We follow Christ not only to "do the right thing" but because Christ is the image in whom we are created. By imitating Christ, each of us becomes the expressed likeness of Christ through transformation in grace; that is, the human person becomes a sacrament of God. By our imitating Christ God truly becomes present in our lives and in our world. To imitate Christ, therefore, is to bring to life the form or expression of the image (of Christ) in which we are created—to become "Christic."

In mapping out the spiritual journey for Agnes of Prague, Clare indicated that the goal of union with God is imitation (cf. 2 LAg 20). This goal is the same for Francis and Bonaventure as well and supports the claim that imitation of Christ is the fruit of prayer. In all three writers we can say that prayer is a deepening of love in union with God and love shapes what we become. In this way, imitation is not a literal mimicking of Christ; rather, it means becoming the image of the beloved through transformation. Francis himself warned against a literal imitation of Christ and admonished those who simply wanted to recall the good works of Jesus or the saints:

> Let all us consider the Good Shepherd who bore the suffering of the cross to save his sheep. The Lord's sheep followed him in tribulation and persecution, in shame and hunger, in weakness and temptation, and in other ways.... Therefore it is a great shame for us that the saints have accomplished great things and we want only to receive glory and honor by recounting them."[4]

Bonaventure, too, believed that love forges a likeness between the lover and the beloved. Writing to Poor Clare nuns he advised: "...seek nothing, desire nothing, wish for no consolation, other than to be able to die with Christ on the cross. Then you may cry out with the apostle

Paul: 'It is now no longer I that live, but Christ lives in me.'"[5] Bonaventure, like Clare, viewed the Christian vocation as "putting on Christ in one's own life" or becoming "another Christ" through compassionate love. To imitate God and to be restored in the image of God is to attain a depth of compassionate love. It means being totally turned toward God, radically dependent on God, and loving like God as a person who is poor and humble.

For Bonaventure, the cross is the basis of imitating the poor and humble Christ and everyone is called to contemplate this image. Francis became "another Christ" because he followed the poor and humble Christ on the cross. "In all things," Bonaventure states, "he wished to be conformed to Christ crucified who hung on the cross poor, suffering and naked."[6] Praying in union with the Crucified led Francis to recognize his dependency on God and others. He became conformed to the Crucified to such a degree that at the end of his life he appeared *like* the Crucified with the wounds of Christ engraved into his flesh. Celano recounts how, after his death, one of the brothers had a dream of Francis but could not tell if the figure he saw was Francis or Christ. Celano writes,

> He appeared to him clothed in a purple dalmatic and followed by an innumerable crowd of people. Several separated themselves from the crowd and said to that brother: "Is this not Christ, brother?" And he replied: "It is he." Others asked him again, saying: "Isn't this Saint Francis?" And the brother likewise replied that it was he. For it really seemed to that brother, and to the whole crowd, as if Christ and Saint Francis were one person.[7]

Bonaventure, too, described Francis as one in whom the life of Christ was renewed. Describing the stigmatized Francis descending the mountain of La Verna he wrote: "After true love of Christ transformed the lover into his image…the angelic man Francis came down from the mountain, bearing with him the likeness of the Crucified."[8] In Bonaventure's view Francis became an *alter Christus*, or another Christ, not only because of the Stigmata but because of the way he related to other people and to creation. Francis became a person of mercy, compassion, reconciliation and peace, and he did so by allowing himself to be fully grasped by the compassionate love of the crucified Christ. For the sake of love he spared nothing and gave everything he had to the one he loved. Compassionate love, in Bonaventure's view, shapes us into the image of the beloved for it removes the dross of the image in which we are created and allows this image to shine without.

For Clare, the transforming power of prayer (as a deepening of love) leads to imitation because it leads to a spiritual birth of Christ in one's life. One becomes, in Clare's words, like Mary "who gave birth to a Son whom the heavens could not contain, and yet she carried him in the little enclosure of her holy womb and held him on her virginal lap."[9] The image of Mary in Clare's writings is not a devotional one; rather, Mary is the exemplar of Christian life, the one who conceived the Word of God and gave birth to a Son "whom the heavens could not contain." She is the model of spiritual motherhood and the perfect imitator of Christ because to become a spiritual mother is what imitation is all about.

The idea of spiritual motherhood was popular among both men and women in the Middle Ages. Bernard of Clairvaux spoke of the Abbot as "Mother"[10] and Francis described himself as a mother to his brothers. In his *Letter to Brother Leo* he wrote: "I am speaking, my son, in this way—as a mother would—because I am putting everything we said on the road in this brief message and advice."[11] To be a mother and to give birth to Jesus in one's life is summed up in Francis' *Later Admonition and Exhortation*: "We are spouses when the faithful soul is united by the Holy Spirit to our Lord Jesus Christ. We are brothers, moreover, when we do the will of His Father who is in heaven; *mothers* when we carry Him in our heart and body through love and a pure and sincere conscience; and give Him birth through a holy activity, which must shine before others by example."[12] To give birth to Christ, for Francis [and Clare], is to let the love that is in our hearts shine through in our lives. When love transforms our actions in a way that Christ is "represented"—then we become mothers, sisters and brothers of Christ.

This birthing of Christ in the life of the believer, as the fruit of prayer, allows us to speak of a "mysticism of motherhood." It is a way of conceiving, birthing and bringing Christ to the world in such a way that the Incarnation is renewed. It is making the gospel alive. We may outline the stages that lead to the imitation or "birth" of Christ in the believer as follows:

MOTHERHOOD	CLARE
Conception	Gaze
Gestation	Consider
Birthing	Contemplate
Nurturing	Imitate

Motherhood for Francis and Clare was more than a physical matter and more than a woman's prerogative. In contemplating Mary's motherhood, Francis and Clare understood their own call to the mystery of motherhood. In his "Salutation of Mary" Francis exclaimed: "Hail his palace! Hail his tabernacle! Hail his dwelling! Hail his robe! Hail his servant! Hail his mother!"[13] Francis understood that Incarnation takes place first and foremost in the human person. Bonaventure, too, indicated that the responsibility for birthing Christ belongs to all "devout souls." He wrote:

> Once this birth has taken place, the devout soul knows and tastes how good is the Lord Jesus. In truth we find how good he is when we nourish him with our prayers, bathe him in the waters of our warm and loving tears, wrap him in the spotless swaddling clothes of our desires, carry him in an embrace of holy love, kiss him over and over again with heartfelt longing and cherish him in the bosom of our inmost heart.[14]

Clare suggests that "gazing" is the beginning stage of giving birth to Christ. When one gazes with all one's heart and soul on the image of the crucified Christ, the image eventually fades, the veil is torn and the door is opened to create a new space for "the other." It was Francis' *embrace of poverty* that prepared the space in his deepest center to receive and carry the Word of God. The beginning of the *Soul's Journey* captures this idea by proposing that no one can begin the journey into God until he is like "the poor one crying in the desert." The soul in prayer who longs for relationship with God is called to conceive the Christ life but cannot do so unless he or she recognizes his or her need for God and the gift of God's grace. In his *Five Feasts of the Child Jesus* Bonaventure tells of the devout soul who conceives mystically by the gift of grace: "...the heavenly Father by a divine seed, impregnates the soul making it fruitful. The power of the Most High comes upon the soul and overshadows it" (Luke1:35).[15] Although it is a joyous conception, the devout soul who has conceived Christ spiritually will find the disciplines of the early journey demanding, disarming and perhaps even bittersweet. This time of walking in the early morning of faith, marked by shadows of darkness and dim light, will gradually give way to the rising sun of a "heart turned toward God," a heart that ultimately says, "and it is no longer I who live, but is is Christ who lives in me" (Galatians 2:20).

While Francis prepared his heart/womb for "conceiving" the Word by embracing poverty it would take a "significant other," the leper, to set the seal of Christ carried through the time of "gestation" in Francis' innermost being. He moved from the "bitter" experience of conceiving the Word to the "sweetness" of one who carried God within and found God without, in the other. We might say that "gestation of the Word" for Francis was conversion, moving from the "bitter" to the "sweet" experience of God symbolized by the kiss of the leper. To allow the Word of God to take root within the heart is to "make a home and a dwelling place for him who is the Lord God Almighty"[16] and this gestation period of the indwelling Word is one of penance: a) love of neighbor—brother, friend or enemy, b) kenotic self-denial and c) a heart turned ever toward the Lord. For Clare, the time of gestation is likened to "considering the crucified Spouse" which is the second step in her prayer schema (gaze, consider). This consideration leads the one who desires God to perceive the poverty and humility of the Most High incarnate in the crucified Spouse. In Clare's view this means pondering the mystery of God as a coincidence of opposites[17] which scandalizes and fascinates: the King of angels who is wrapped in swaddling clothes;[18] the Most High who rules heaven and earth, yet appears in the world despised, needy and poor;[19] the Son of the Most High who takes refuge in the little cloister of Mary's womb.[20]

Birthing is never easy and it is always a wonder. Francis' spiritual motherhood was shown in the birth he gave to a brotherhood of poor men. Bonaventure linked the motherhood of Mary with that of Francis: "The sons and heirs of the eternal King have been born of a 'poor mother' and by the power of the Holy Spirit and they will be begotten by the spirit of poverty in our poor little Order."[21] According to Bonaventure, motherhood distinguished the life of Francis: "He seemed like a mother who was daily bringing [souls] to birth in Christ."[22] Celano, too, described Francis' love of his brothers as the love of a tender and nurturing mother: "...casting himself at the feet of His Majesty he offered sacrifice of spirit for his sons...he felt compassion and love filled with fear...his spirit had given birth to them with greater labor pains than a mother feels within herself."[23] Clare expressed the birth of Christ in her life by her example of humility and poverty and the outpouring of love she showed to her sisters, calling them to be mirrors and examples of this love to one another and to the world.[24]

The mysticism of motherhood in the lives of Francis and Clare means that the maturity of Franciscan prayer does not stop with union of the individual soul with God. Rather, the goal of prayer is bringing Christ to birth, that is, a union in love with God that conceives the Word, carries the Word, gives birth to the Word and then is mirrored in the Word. This "mysticism of motherhood," as the imitation of Christ, becomes a reality in the life of the believer when the soul can cry out of the Word delivered of her or him: "This is my Body." If, indeed, imitation is the goal of prayer and means bringing Christ to life in the believer, then we would have to concede that the life-giving relationship of prayer is expressed most fully in the Eucharist. We are called to become what we conceive within us in the same way that we are called to become what we love. Gospel life is focused on being a "person in relationship" and a sharing among persons of the experience of Christ.[25] It is bound up with the body of Christ and the bodies of all those who follow Christ. In his book *Swimming in the Sun* Albert Haase writes, "We are the body of Christ on earth and everyday, in some way, we are challenged to become the bread that is broken for the hungry of the world."[26] Eucharist is bread broken and eaten for a hungry world. It is the food that gives the strength to make every stranger beloved. Miroslav Volf writes,

> We would most profoundly misunderstand the Eucharist if we thought of it only as a sacrament of God's embrace of which we are the fortunate beneficiaries. Inscribed in the very heart of God's grace is the rule that we can be its recipients only if we do not resist being made into its agents. What happens to us must be done by us."[27]

To be the body of Christ is not simply a nice spiritual idea—it is a flesh and blood reality. "Christ has no body now but yours," Teresa of Avila once wrote, "no hands but yours, no feet but yours. Yours are the eyes through which must look out Christ's compassion on the world." The words of Teresa echo in the writings of our Franciscan guides, namely, that the body of Christ has no meaning without us. What is the significance of Christ if those who claim belief in Christ do not live in the mystery of Christ? To live in the mystery means what Christ has begun we are called to help complete—not only for the wholeness and healing of humanity but for the sake of the earth and for the entire universe.

Prayer that leads to the imitation of Christ is urgently needed in our world today, although we seem to be far from this goal. Privatism, individualism, consumerism and other "-isms" all work against a public expression of gospel life. On one hand we lament the fragmentation, disparity and abuse in our world, and on the other hand we privatize the fact that we Christians are gospel people. If we truly believed that Christ is the center of our life and world, that each of us is a member of the body of Christ, and that body is incomplete without us, that the fullness of Christ encompasses all peoples, all races, religions and cultures, indeed, the entire universe, would we harm our neighbor? Injure or abuse the earth? Kill our enemies? Ignore the poor, the homeless or the outcasts of our society? If we truly believed that all is Christ, would we continue to crucify Christ? Or would we act according to the law of Jesus: love, mercy and compassion? Would we be willing to lay down our lives out of love for the sake of the other? If we truly believed that Christ is center of the universe, would we be so private about the Good News we hold so sacred? Thomas Merton once wrote that only in union with Christ, who is the fully integrated Person, can one become trans-personal, trans-cultural and trans-social.[28] Only in union with Christ, the One, can a person be united to the many since, as Word and center of the Trinity, Christ is both the One and the Many.

We may not all have the same experience of Christ but each of us is called to live in the mystery of Christ in our own lives, to express this mystery through our gifts, talents, personality, to participate in the larger mystery of Christ to which we are called. As Zachary Hayes writes, "we are not to become carbon copies of this historical Jesus nor of Francis nor of anyone else. We are to fill the Christ-form with the elements of our own personal life and thus embody something of the Word in ourselves in a distinctive and personal way."[29] To live in the body of Christ today is to follow Christ in an evolutionary universe, to harness the energies of love so that the universe itself becomes more visibly the body of Christ, a body of complexity and diversity united in love. Each of us has a distinct role in the Christ mystery and the fullness of the mystery of Christ is either enhanced or diminished by the degree of our participation. It may seem far-fetched to suggest this idea but the science of quantum theory can help us understand our role in the Christ mystery.

The science of quantum physics tells us that we live in a participatory universe where the observer determines reality. Our participation in the universe is what makes it real and alive. Without us the universe makes no real sense. In the same way, we may think of the mystery of Christ as a participative mystery. Our participation in Christ is necessary to make Christ alive. Without us the mystery of Christ makes no sense. Prayer leads us into the mystery of Christ by opening us up to this mystery in our lives. To become a "Christic" person is to come to a new level of personhood, a transcendent level, by which we realize that the God whose goodness permeates our lives, also lives in our brothers and sisters. Therefore, we humans are not like separate atoms in the universe. Rather the goodness of God in me is also in my neighbor; thus I am incomplete apart from my neighbor who is my brother and sister. If I am to find God then I must gaze on my neighbor who is a mirror of Christ. If I am to come to the fullness of who I am I must love my neighbor in whom I dwell and who is something of me. To come to this new level of personhood is to contemplate Christ, to penetrate the truth of the Christ mystery in the community of humankind. Christ comes to be the fullness of the universe when we become the fullness of Christ. The contemporary writer and Teilhard scholar, Beatrice Bruteau, describes the mystery of Christ for our time in a way that reflects the thought of Bonaventure. She writes,

> To enter by our transcendent freedom into Christ and to become a new creation means to enter by faith into the future of every person and into the very heart of creativity itself, into the future of God....To be "in Christ" is to abandon thinking of oneself only in terms of categories and abstractions by which one may be externally related to others and to coincide with oneself as a transcendent center of energy that lives in God and in one's fellows—because that is where the Christ lives, in God and in us. To be "in Christ" is to experience oneself as an initiative of free energy radiating out to give life abundantly to all, for that is the function of Christ. To be "in Christ" is to be an indispensable member of a living body which is the Body of Christ. To be "in Christ" is to be identified with the Living One who is not to be sought among the dead, for the Living One is the One who is Coming to Be.[30]

Living in a Christic world in which the whole is the body of Christ is not a matter of waiting for theologians to write new books or develop new insights. It is a matter of living in the mystery itself. A dynamic living relationship with God is what prayer is all about, and only when this relationship is active and alive does Christ become active and alive in our lives and in our world. This is what the early Franciscans did and what we are called to do today. It is what Francis asked of his disciples before his death when he said, "I have done what is mine to do. May Christ teach you yours."[31]

If we become too privatized in our culture and too sedentary in our ways to really live the Christ mystery in its fullness, then the world fails to hear and see the Good News of God among us. Prayer that leads to the imitation of Christ calls for a type of public witness that demands our full participation—heart, mind, body and soul. When we allow ourselves to be grasped by God fully then gospel living becomes radical living. Our hearts centered in God cannot help but see God incarnate in every person, creature, flower, earthworm and tree. As we see, so we love. If we begin to see differently—if we begin to see that all of creation is in some way incarnational—then we begin to love differently. And the way we love can change the world. If we dare to follow this path of prayer to the imitation of Christ, we must be ready to move from the center of comfort to the margins of conflict because that is where the body of Christ grows fastest. Can we pray so as to live in the fullness of the mystery of Christ, believing that every person regardless of race, religion or creed, belongs to Christ? Can we live in the mystery that all things are in Christ and Christ is in all things, and that loving our neighbor in Christ is the path to unity in God? Such unity extends not only to our brothers and sisters of other cultures, religions and languages but to the earth itself, recognizing that we and the earth are on the journey to God together. Solidarity with all people and solidarity with the earth are signs of those living in the fullness of the body of Christ. The key to solidarity is finding Christ at the center of our lives so that we may recognize Christ as the center of others' lives, the center of the earth and the center of the universe.

Prayer that leads to imitation must be passionate, for passionate prayer expresses itself in the believer. When we come to the fullness of God's life within us then we become the body of Christ in the world. Christ lives insofar as we live in him and in the fullness of who we are. Thus nothing is to hinder us, nothing is to come between us and the love of Christ, nothing else is worth our energies than to allow Christ to live in us. The body of Christ grows as we become mothers, sisters or brothers and spouses of Christ, but it remains diminished insofar as we fail to live up to our Christian vocation. Imitation is what makes the Good News of God among us visible and alive, resounding into the vast corners of the universe; the Good News that every single person, creature, star and element has been loved by God into being and is destined for eternal life with God, a life of communion in love.

Bonaventure claimed that the meaning of the cosmos is concentrated in humanity and radicalized in the person of Jesus Christ. Christ is not ordained to us, he wrote, rather, we are ordained to Christ. The whole of creation is made for Christ. And since the whole is made for Christ, it is not surprising that through his resurrection, Christ shares life with all creation. In Bonaventure's words:

> All things are said to be transformed in the transfiguration of Christ, in as far as something of each creature was transfigured in Christ. For as a human being, Christ has something in common with all creatures. With the stone he shares existence; with plants he shares life; with animals he shares sensation; and with the angels he shares intelligence. Therefore, all things are said to be transformed in Christ since—in his human nature—he embraces something of every creature in himself when he is transfigured.[32]

If, as Bonaventure suggests, Christ embodies the whole of creation in his individual nature then all of creation (and not just humanity) is transformed in the presence of the living God. Zachary Hayes writes, "what happened between God and the world in Christ points to the future of the cosmos. It is a future that involves the radical transformation of creation reality through the unitive power of God's creative love."[33] The justice and peace that we long for in our world, therefore, must also be a justice and peace of the earth, a justice of relationship with the natural elements, with ecosystems and rain forests, with all creatures of creation. For in the end (whatever that physical end will be) the earth will not be annihilated or destroyed but together with humanity will be transformed in the love of God. What we hope for (and what guides our lives) is a new heaven and earth with Christ as center, a center of love, happiness and peace.

Giving ourselves to the cause of Christ is not to lose the world but to find the world in its truest reality in its deepest relation to God. We are the body of Christ and each day we are called to live in the body to its fullest, not only for our own healing and wholeness, but for the transformation of the universe. Prayer is that living relationship of love whereby we come to a new level of consciousness of ourselves and our world and start attracting a new reality—the consciousness that God is with us, that Christ lives at the heart of the world, and that every person, creature, plant, tree and element of the universe is, in some way, related to Christ. Jesus Christ is risen and shares life with us as crucified and glorified. There is no wound or sorrow that has not been lifted up into the embrace of God's eternal love. Yet, the wholeness of earth we seek between peoples, cultures, races, religions and the environment remains incomplete, for the fullness of Christ is incomplete. We are the body of Christ and until Christ's body becomes our body, all of creation will continue to groan aloud in the pangs of new birth. Only prayer can lead us into the mystery of Christ and open our hearts to the wonder of God.

Meditation

For Francis, the life of penance (as difficult as it is) is meant to bring Christ to birth in the life of the believer. Meditate on the following words of Francis and see how they apply to your own life.

> We are spouses when the faithful soul is united by the Holy Spirit to our Lord Jesus Christ. We are brothers, moreover, when we do the will of his Father who is in heaven; mothers when we carry him in our heart and body through love and a pure and sincere conscience; and give him birth through a holy activity, which must shine before others by example." (*Later Admonition and Exhortation*)

Keeping in mind the words of Francis, see how they challenge you to grow in light of the following questions:

1. How do you see yourself as an "image of Christ"?
2. What are several ways Christians can enter more fully into the Christ mystery?
3. Are you willing to publicly witness to Jesus Christ? If so, what does this mean to you?
4. How can prayer lead you to imitation of Christ?

NOTES

[1] Peter Casarella, "The Expression and Form of the Word: Trinitarian Hermeneutics and the Sacramentality of Language in Hans Urs Von Balthasar's Theology," *Renascence* 48.2 (Winter, 1996): 114–115.

[2] Peter Casarella, "Experience as a Theological Category: Hans Urs von Balthasar on the Christian Encounter with God's Image," *Communio* 20 (Spring, 1993): 124.

[3] Casarella, "Expression and Form," 128.

[4] Francis of Assisi, *Admonition* 6 (*Écrits*, 100). Engl. trans. *FA:ED* I, 131.

[5] Bonaventure, *Perf. Vit.* 6.2 (VIII, 120). Engl. trans. De Vinck, "On Perfection of Life," 239–40; cf. Gal 2:20.

[6] Bonaventure, *Leg. maj.* 14.4 (*EM*, 117). Engl. trans. *FA:ED* II, 642. See also "Sermon on Feast of Transferal" where Bonaventure writes: "he was made utterly Christ-like and configured to him." Engl. trans. *FA:ED* II, 745.

[7] Celano, "Remembrance of the Desire of a Soul," 165. Engl. trans. *FA:ED* II, 389.

[8] Bonaventure, *Leg. maj.* 13.5 (*EM*, 109). Engl. trans. *FA:ED* II, 634.

[9] Clare of Assisi, 3 *LAg* 18–19 (*Écrits*, 104). Engl. trans. Armstrong, *Clare of Assisi: Early Documents*, 46. I am indebted here to Thelma Steiger whose paper on mystical motherhood in Clare and Francis was influential on this section.

[10] See Caroline Walker Bynum, *Jesus as Mother: Studies in the Spirituality of the High Middle Ages* (Berkeley, CA: University of California Press, 1982), 110–169, especially pp. 116, 155.

[11] Francis of Assisi, "Letter to Brother Leo" (*Écrits*, 266). Engl. trans. *FA:ED* I, 122.

[12] Francis of Assisi, *Later Admonition and Exhortation* 51–53 (*Écrits*, 236). Engl. trans. *FA:ED* I, 49.

[13] Francis of Assisi, "A Salutation of the Blessed Virgin Mary" (*Écrits*, 274). Engl. trans. *FA:ED* I, 163.

[14] Bonaventure, "The Five Feasts of the Child Jesus," in *Bonaventure: Mystic of God's Word*, ed. Timothy Johnson (New York: New City Press, 1999), 145.

[15] Bonaventure, "Five Feasts of the Child Jesus," 140.

[16] Francis of Assisi, *Earlier Rule* 22.27 (*Écrits*, 166).

[17] The "coincidence of opposites" is a structure of thought by which opposites exist simultaneously. It is interesting that Clare shows evidence of this thought in her writings, since it is Bonaventure who most frequently used the coincidence of opposites to describe the mystery of Christ. For a full discussion on the coincidence of opposites see Ewert Cousins, *Bonaventure and the Coincidence of Opposites* (Chicago: Franciscan Herald Press, 1978); ibid., "The Coincidence of Opposites in the Christology of Saint Bonaventure," *Franciscan Studies* 28 (1968): 27–45.

[18] Clare of Assisi, 4 *LAg* 19–21 (*Écrits*, 114).

[19] Clare of Assisi, 1 *LAg* 19 (*Écrits*, 86-88).

[20] Clare of Assisi, 3 *LAg* 17–19 (*Écrits*, 104).

[21] Bonaventure, *Leg. maj.* 3.10 (*EM*, 27). Engl. trans. *FA:ED* II, 548.

[22] Bonaventure, *Leg. maj.* 8.1 (*EM*, 64). Engl. trans. *FA:ED* II, 587.

[23] Thomas of Celano, "Remembrance of the Desire of a Soul," 132. Engl. trans. *FA:ED* II, 359.

[24] Clare of Assisi, *Testament* (*Écrits*, 168–170) 19–22. Engl. trans. Armstrong, *Clare of Assisi: Early Documents*, 57.

[25] Chinnici, "Evangelical and Apostolic Tensions," 7.

[26] Albert Haase, *Swimming in the Sun: Discovering the Lord's Prayer with Francis of Assisi and Thomas Merton* (Cincinnati: St. Anthony Messenger Press, 1993), 144.

[27] Volf, *Exclusion and Embrace*, 129.

[28] William Thompson, *Jesus, Lord and Savior: A Theopatic Christology and Soteriology* (New York: Paulist, 1980), 250–71; ibid., "The Risen Christ, Transcultural Consciousness, and the Encounter of the World Religions," *Theological Studies* 37 (1976): 399–405.

[29] Zachary Hayes, "Christ, Word of God and Exemplar of Humanity," *Cord* 46.1 (1996): 15.

[30] Beatrice Bruteau, *The Grand Option: Personal Transformation and a New Creation* (Notre Dame, IN: University of Notre Dame Press, 2001), 172–73.

[31] Bonaventure, *Leg. maj.* 14.3 (*EM*, 117). Engl. trans. *FA:ED* II, 642.

[32] Bonaventure, *Sermo I, Dom. II in Quad.* (IX, 215–219). Engl. trans. Hayes, "Christ, Word of God and Exemplar of Humanity," 13.

[33] Hayes, "Christ, Word of God and Exemplar of Humanity," 12.

Chapter Nine

THE WAY TO PEACE

I call upon the Eternal Father
Through his Son, our Lord Jesus Christ,
That through the intercession of the most holy Virgin Mary,
The mother of the same God and Lord Jesus Christ,
And through the intercession of blessed Francis,
Our leader and father,
He may enlighten the eyes of our soul
To guide our feet
In the way of that peace
Which surpasses all understanding.
This is the peace
Proclaimed and given to us by our Lord Jesus Christ
And preached again and again
By our father Francis.
At the beginning and end of every sermon he announced peace;
In every greeting he wished for peace;
In every contemplation he sighed for ecstatic peace—
Like a citizen of that Jerusalem of which
That Man of Peace says,
Who was peaceable with those who hated peace;
Pray for the peace of Jerusalem.

—Bonaventure
The Soul's Journey into God

There is no doubt that we live in a time of war and violence. Despite the rhetoric of democracy, mutuality and globalization, the reality is imperialism, domination and oppression. The gap between the rich and poor continues to widen. This lament does not detract from the fact that there are millions committed to peace, reflected in bumper stickers and front lawn signs: "make peace not war," "let peace reign," "there is no way to peace, peace is the way." Peace, of course, cannot be really "made"; rather, it must be embodied. It is first of all a personal spirituality before it is a political reality. The Franciscan path of prayer leads to peace because it is a path of active love. It is opening the mind and heart to the grace of God, and allowing God's grace to touch the deepest core of one's being. The path to peace means undergoing conversion in the deepest core of one's self and finding one's true self in God. It is a path of relationship with God that is centered on the Word made flesh, the person of Jesus Christ. Christ not only reveals God to us but Christ is the union of divine and human where the fullest possibilities of human life are joined with the fullness of God.

Francis of Assisi encountered the God of peace in the crucified Christ because he encountered the God of compassionate love. Peace is the unity of love. God is true peace because God is Trinity—giving, receiving and sharing love. Love that is given, received and shared requires a community of persons in a union of love; it requires the deepest level of relationship. God is peace because God is a communion of love. Too often we make peace a commodity, a "thing" to obtain, an abstraction, a category. Too little do we understand peace as a spiritual way of union, as a communion of love. Peace is relational—like God— and does not exist without community. Where there is God there is love and where there is love there is peace.

To be a peacemaker is to accept the gift of peace given to us by Jesus Christ, that is, to accept God's love in Christ, a gift which is given to us in the wounds of the crucified Christ. God's love given to us in Christ, the gift of peace, is a gift graciously given through suffering. To accept this gift, we must descend with Christ into the suffering of humanity, to accept our own woundedness and then to acknowledge our wounding of others. The love that brings peace, according to Bonaventure, is the acceptance of woundedness for *the sake of others*, ultimately, loving the other by way of self-gift.[1] To live in this spirit of love is to live as image of God, and to live as image of God is to live as image of peace because God's image is peace made visible to us in the crucified Christ. The contemporary peacemaker and spiritual writer, Walter Wink, claims that "Christians are to be nonviolent not simply because it 'works,' but because it reflects the very nature of God."[2] The peace that we long for is the peace of the image of God. For Clare of Assisi, prayer helps us disclose this image of peace within us because prayer unlocks the door to the heart.

Because the gift of peace is given to us by Christ, peace is decisively incarnational. It centers on the human person. Francis of Assisi had profound insight with regard to the human person whom he viewed as the source of both violence and peace. Francis believed that peace begins in the heart. "As you announce peace with your mouth, make sure that you have greater peace in your hearts. . . . Let everyone be drawn to peace and kindness through your peace and gentleness."[3] Yet, he recognized that violence also begins in the human heart because the heart joined to the will has the freedom to choose. It was perhaps in his encounter with the leper that Francis confronted the violence within him. His sense of horror made him realize that he must first conquer himself if he was to overcome his fear of those he rejected—the lepers. Francis had to undergo an inward liberation through release of self. That is, peace was not something he acquired through a renunciation of possessions or because he stopped fighting with others. Rather, peace was a way of being, a spiritual attitude. The peace that Francis sought required a change of heart. "In all of his preaching," Celano writes, "he prayed for peace saying, 'May the Lord give you peace'....Many who hated peace along with salvation, with the Lord's help [and Francis' example] came to embrace peace."[4]

For Francis peace was not just the absence of conflict or the tranquility of order but the peace the Gospel speaks of: peace at the core and center of one's being. His simple act of praying with attention, turning his mind and heart to God, helped him grow in awareness of who God was and who he was, and in this awareness he found the energy of transformation both for himself and the world around him. Such awareness lessened his need for frantic control and manipulation. Rather, he accepted himself as part of the problem (of sinful humanity) and strove to realize his dependency on his brothers and sisters and all of creation, realizing his poverty of being human. If we seek peace through external means—money, weapons, power—we simply prolong the inevitability of war and violence. Peace is not an abstract concept; it is not a universal ideal. Francis understood that worldly peace brings war because worldly peace is a false peace in which persons can be in serious sin, tranquil about their vices and unaware of structures that oppress and dominate. To have world peace we must first have peace within ourselves. The idea of "world peace" is abstract unless each person strives for inner peace, and this means opening ourselves to the transforming action of God's Spirit within us. As Francis grew in the love of God, he became a man of peace, becoming more sensitive to and critical of those solutions which, in the end, did not foster true peace, such as the battles between Assisi and neighboring towns. He came to see that peace flows from the river of prayer because it is the grace of the Spirit which seeps into the human heart. Francis' mission of peace was not one of protest or demonstration; rather, he sent the brothers out to announce peace *and* penance: "Go, my dear brothers two by two through different parts of the word, *announcing peace to the people and penance for the remission of sins.*"[5] Because we are all capable of violence, we are all in need of continual conversion.

Francis lived a life of poverty, penance and conversion, following the example of Jesus Christ, so that he could overcome his violent self and become a human-loving person. His desire for God was nurtured by the Spirit of unceasing prayer, and to have this Spirit was to be free of those things which possessed him and prevented him from loving God. Prayer is the cry of the poor one in the desert who is far from home and recognizes the need for God. Francis realized that the Spirit of love cannot take root in a heart that is possessed by other things:

anger, hurt, jealousy or material possessions. Only a heart turned toward God can freely welcome the Spirit of love and provide room within for the Spirit to dwell. This indwelling Spirit is the basis of friendship with Christ that begins with the gaze on the crucified Lover. True friendship means sharing the joys and sorrows of life. Thus to become a friend of Christ is to share the bitterness and sweetness of loving Christ. Penance and conversion are necessary to overcome inner structures of violence because only when the human heart is converted from violence to nonviolence, from inner war to inner peace, can one be a friend of Christ. Penance that leads to friendship with Christ welcomes the Spirit of Christ. Nonviolence is the Spirit of God that disarms our hearts so that we can become God's instruments for the disarmament of the world.[6]

Prayer is the path to peace because it is the path to love, not to a "feel good" love but to compassionate love, the type of love that can reach out and feel for another and give itself to the other without asking for anything in return. It is in prayer that we encounter Jesus who is our peace and learn from him the way to peace. One of the most noted peacemakers of our time, Daniel Berrigan, wrote that "the soul of peacemaking is the will to give one's life."[7] Bonaventure, too, saw that there is no other way to peace than through the burning love of the Crucified. Union with God is a union in love whereby one is inflamed with the desire of crucified love. In this union of love, a person is willing to suffer or die out of love for another, following the example of Christ.

The Spirit of prayer that leads to compassionate love must reach down into the depths of our humanity and search these depths in the mirror of the crucified Christ. Clare's template of evangelical prayer paves the way to peace because we are asked to find our identity, our "face" in the mirror of the crucified Christ—to come to the truth of who we are. The gaze on the Crucified is the gaze on our own humanity. Poverty frees us so that we may gaze more deeply on the God of compassionate love who comes to us in wounded humanity—our own humanity as well as the fragile humanity of our brothers and sisters. We are to first see in the mirror of the Crucified that each of us is loved in a unique and particular way. Only the person who is poor and humble can accept God's unconditional love and embrace. To accept God's love in humility is to admit in the mirror of the Crucified—"what I am I am before you and in you, and by accepting who I am, I accept your love for me, your love which has created me and continues to recreate me."

Prayer that leads to self-knowledge is liberating because then we can accept God's love where we are and we can begin to accept who we are in view of God's overflowing love. This spiraling dynamic of love— into the heart of the self and into the heart of God—is the birth of peace in the seeker of peace because it is the birth of peace in the lover of God. Clare's profound insight with regard to self-identity and contemplation plays an important role in this dynamic. When we come to an honest acceptance of ourselves and God's love for us, she indicates, when we study our face in the mirror of the cross and allow God's grace to touch us and transform us, then we begin to see the world around us—our neighbors, our community—with contemplative vision.

We cannot gaze upon the crucified Christ and come to a level of contemplation without ultimately being transformed. According to Clare, we give ourselves—heart, mind and soul—to God, so that God's grace may transform us into vessels of compassionate love. Francis became a man of peace because he was transformed in love and came to recognize that he was intimately related (*pietas*) to every person and creature.[8] We see in the life of Francis that peace extended to all of creation. Francis came to realize his "family" relatedness to everything, including the tiny creatures of creation. Bonaventure writes,

> True piety had so filled Francis' heart and penetrated its depths that it seemed to have claimed the man of God completely into its dominion.[9] This is what, through devotion, lifted him up to God; through compassion, transformed him into Christ; through self-emptying, turned him to his neighbor; through universal reconciliation with each thing, refashioned him to the state of innocence.[10]

Francis' piety was the fruit of his ongoing conversion. It was the source of his reverence for animals and he recognized them as fellow creatures and signs of Christ. Celano writes: "That the bees not perish of hunger in the icy winter, he commands that honey and the finest wine should be set out for them. He calls all animals by a fraternal name, although, among all kinds of beasts, he especially loves the meek."[11] The notion of *cortesia* or deferential behavior characterized Francis' respect for creation, including the natural elements, even fire. He made use of chivalric values to express his unique ideas of spiritual honor and deference between all the levels of creation. Celano writes,

> Even for worms he had a warm love, since he had read this text about the Savior: I am a worm and not a man. That is why he used to pick them up from the road and put them in a safe place so that they would not be crushed by the footsteps of passersby....Whenever he found an abundance of flowers, he used to preach to them and invite them to praise the Lord, just as if they were endowed with reason.[12]

The life of Francis gave new meaning to the divine command of dominion found in the book of Genesis (1:28). He did not consider himself at the top of a hierarchy of being nor did he declare himself superior to the non-human creation. Rather, Francis saw himself as part of creation. His spirituality overturned the spirituality of hierarchical ascent and replaced it with a spirituality of descending solidarity between humanity and all of creation.[13] That is, instead of using creatures to ascend to God (in a transcending manner), he found God in all creatures and identified with them as brother and sister. Bonaventure writes "he would call creatures, no matter how small by the name of "brother" or "sister" because he knew they shared with him the same beginning."[14] By surrendering himself and daring everything for love's sake, the earth became his home and all creatures his brothers and sisters. That led him to love and respect the world around him and made him truly a man of peace.

Only prayer, the Spirit of God breathing in us, dwelling in our hearts and joining us to Christ, can lead us, like Francis, to the contemplative vision of God's goodness in every creature and in every living thing. Contemplative vision brings peace because it is the type of vision that recognizes "I am in you and you are in me because we both have the same source of life, the God of overflowing love." If God is the source of my life and the source of your life as well, then the fullness of my life can only be found in you and in all that is in this world, because the fullness of God is expressed in humanity and all of creation. This is the vision that recognizes we are not isolated or fragmented parts but that we are all one; therefore, it is the vision that sees the other and welcomes the other in an embrace. Contemplative vision is the vision that says "you are good *as you are* because you are the sacrament of God's love." This type of vision, therefore, leads us to the truth that all reality expresses the goodness of God. By seeing this goodness and loving the goodness of the other we begin to live in peace.

The Franciscan way to peace is the path to transformation that passes through the crucible of love because it is a "yes" to the embrace of the crucified Christ. Here is the challenge of being Christian and the test of whether or not we really are Christian. The one who prays along the path of Franciscan prayer must be led to ask, do I really believe in Christ crucified as the revelation of God's love for me? Am I willing to follow the way of the cross? Because to pray with open hearts to a God of compassionate love who died on a cross and who desires to embrace us from the cross is dangerous, costly and perhaps even fatal. The Franciscan path of prayer is not platonic, it does not seek another world above or blissful spiritual union detached from ugly, suffering flesh. On the contrary, Franciscan prayer plunges us into the depths of humanity with its wounds, its leprosy, its violence and abuse. We are led by the Spirit to descend with Christ into the darkness and loneliness of humanity, and are asked to love like Christ with the costly ointment of our lives. "Unless a grain of wheat falls into the earth and dies," Jesus said, "it remains just a single grain; but if it dies, it bears much fruit" (John 12:24). Francis realized that peacemaking involves pardoning, bearing infirmities and tribulation, and suffering in the right spirit for love of God. In his *Admonition* on peacemaking he wrote, "true peacemakers are those who preserve peace of mind and body for love of our Lord Jesus Christ, despite what they suffer in this world."[15] He was keenly aware that true peacemakers are those who are willing to suffer for peace and to endure in peace. "Praised be you my Lord through those who give pardon for Your love, and bear infirmity and tribulation. Blessed are they who endure in peace, for by You, Most High they shall be crowned."[16] Bonaventure draws a parallel between Francis the peacemaker and Francis the "other Christ" (*alter Christus*). Only someone conformed to Christ, who puts on Christ and thus, in whom Christ lives, is a peacemaker because that person is willing to suffer or die like Christ for the sake of peace. Francis was a peacemaker because he bore the wounds of Christ, that is, his depth of compassionate love for others was such that he spent himself completely for the other in love.

Death is not appealing to us and our culture constantly fights against it. Yet, death is integral to the Christian path of peace because it is the path of life. Death yields to life—this is the heart of the Christian message. Christ has conquered death and has risen to new life. The last word, therefore, is *life*. However, the path to life goes first through the cross of suffering. The noted philosopher of environmental ethics, Holmes Rolston III, states that all of creation is cruciform. "This whole evolutionary upslope," he writes, "is a calling in which renewed life comes by blasting the old. Life is gathered up in the midst of its throes, a blessed tragedy, lived in grace through a besetting storm."[17] In one of his lectures on the *Six Days of Creation* Bonaventure said that Christ has to suffer in his mystical body before there will be peace in the world and, we might add, creation.[18] Francis reached the age of peace because he was conformed to Christ crucified—Christ suffered in Francis' body—and he expressed this union (with Christ) in a spirit of compassionate love. We, too, are asked to "re-present" Christ through compassionate love, to breathe that Spirit of God so deeply within us that we can say with Paul: "For through the law I died to the law, so that I might live to God. I have been crucified with Christ" (Galatians 2:19). This is the way to peace.

The symbol of peace for Francis was the Eucharist. In his *Letter to the Entire Order* he wrote: "I implore you brothers to show all possible reverence and honor to the most holy Body and Blood of our Lord Jesus Christ in whom that which is in heaven and on earth has been brought to peace and reconciled to almighty God."[19] Being a peacemaker means living a eucharistic life, the life of Christ. To live in the Eucharist is to live in the body of Christ—the body that refuses to keep bodies separate but unites them through suffering love; it is to live in the spirit of crucified love. Miroslav Volf states that since the body of Christ lives as a complex interplay of differentiated bodies, following the Crucified does not mean moving from the particularity of the body to the universality of the Spirit but from separated bodies to the community of interrelated bodies—the one body in the Spirit with many discrete members.[20] The Spirit breaks through the self-enclosed worlds we inhabit, recreates us and sets us on the road toward new creation. "A catholic personality is a personality enriched by otherness," Volf writes. The Spirit unlatches the door of one's heart saying, "You are not only you; others belong to you too."[21] A catholic personality, therefore, requires a catholic community. Each one must say, "I am not only I; all others belong to me too." This is Francis and Clare's thought as well. Community is formed by bonds of love and sacrifice, as a mother loves her son. The heart of the Christian life, centered in the cross, involves creating space in oneself for the other to come in. Volf states that when God sets out to embrace the enemy, the result is the cross. On the cross the dancing circle of self-giving and mutually indwelling Trinitarian persons of love opens up for the enemy. We are embraced by the divine persons who love us with the same love in which they love each other and who make space for us within their own eternal embrace.[22] Just as the arms of the crucified Christ are a sign of a space in God's self and an invitation for the enemy to come in, so too are we to do the same.[23]

Eucharist is ritual time in which we celebrate this divine "making space for us and inviting us in." What happens to us must be done by us. Having been embraced by God, we must make space for others in ourselves and invite them in—even our enemies.[24] In receiving Christ's broken body and blood we in a sense receive all those whom Christ received through his suffering. The other of embrace is not just the brother or sister inside the self-enclosed ecclesial community. The other is also the enemy outside us. All are taken into the embrace by being forgiven and called "brother" and "sister." We who have been embraced by the outstretched arms of the crucified God open our arms even for our enemies, to make space in ourselves for them and to invite them in, so that together we may rejoice in the eternal embrace of the triune God.[25]

Crucified love is love that creates a new future because it is the love that makes space for the other to enter in and share life. This is the love of salvation because it is the love of healing that restores unity and peace. It is the love of community because it recognizes that the wholeness of community requires healing in the midst of wounded, broken bodies. To love in the spirit of crucified love, to let this love be shown in the "birthing" of Christ, is to create a new future of life, a future of healing wounds, divisions, hatred and animosity, the healing that brings peace. Beatrice Bruteau writes: "If we really accept that creation is always new, and if we ourselves are active participants in this new creation, then we are always facing the future."[26] If we desire a future of unity and peace then we must participate in the path of salvation that brings together that which is divided. Christ crucified is the way to peace. In Celano's view, Francis' life was Eucharistic because his was the body of Christ given over to others in a spirit of forgiveness and reconciliation, and for the sake of unity and peace.[27] The parallel Celano draws between the wounded body of Francis and the wounded body of Christ is no mere piety. Rather, in Celano's view, only a wounded body can bring about the peace and healing of reconciling love. Francis himself wrote that to follow Christ is to follow the Good Shepherd who laid down his life for his sheep (cf. *Adm* 6). He believed that we must follow the footprints of Christ and love to the point of death if we wish to attain eternal life. A person can live in the spirit of crucified love, however, only when he or she *believes* that he or she is loved. "The root of Christian love," Merton wrote, "is not the will to love, but *the faith that one is loved*."[29] To live in the spirit of crucified Christ is to live in the trust of God's fidelity, God's "I love you, I am with you," in the human heart. This faithful love of God empowers us to give birth to Christ. It makes us free to face our enemies and those who hate us because it makes us free to see the goodness of God in the mirror of wounded bodies and souls—those who we would otherwise reject, as Francis first rejected the leper.

We are all aware of the world's violence today, the hatred, anger and hurt of human lives, and the abuse inflicted on mother earth. However, are we aware as Christians that all forms of violence are wounds inflicted on Christ's body and that Christ is crucified again and again? In his book, *New Seeds of Contemplation* Thomas Merton wrote,

> All over the face of the earth the avarice and lust of men breed unceasing divisions among them, and the wounds that tear men from union with one another widen and open out into huge wars. Murder, massacres, revolution, hatred, the slaughter and torture of the bodies and souls of men, the destruction of cities by fire, the starvation of millions, the annihilation of populations and finally the cosmic inhumanity of atomic war: Christ is massacred in his members, torn limb from limb; God is murdered in men.[30]

What is perhaps difficult to admit is that Christians play a part in the constant violence of our world—the massacre of Christ—a part that (actively) condones violence by our silence, apathy and privatism—in short, an unwillingness to be "other Christs." Some members of the institutional church preach Christ yet fail to live the mystery of Christ. It exists as an accommodating church that seeks prestige without the pain of the cross, a church that hides under the blanket of other-worldliness.[31] One of the great peacemakers of our time, Martin Luther King, Jr., was arrested in Birmingham, Alabama, on Good Friday 1963 for demanding racial justice. In his "Letter from a Birmingham Jail," King responded to those who criticized him and expressed his hope and disappointment in the church:

> I have watched so many churches commit themselves to a completely otherworldly religion which made a strange distinction between body and soul, the sacred and the secular. So here we are moving toward the exit of the twentieth century with a religious community largely adjusted to the status quo, standing as a taillight behind other community agencies rather than a headlight leading men and women to

higher levels of justice....In deep disappointment, I have
wept over the laxity of the church. But be assured that my
tears have been tears of love. There can be no deep disappointment where there is not deep love....Yes, I love the
church....Yes, I see the church as the body of Christ. But,
oh! How we have blemished and scarred that body through
social neglect and fear of being nonconformists.[32]

The Franciscan path of prayer that leads to peace takes this world seriously because we believe that God dwells among us and lives with us
crucified and glorified. But if we pray—if we really pray—then we must
forget about ourselves and throw ourselves into the mercy of God
because to pray to a crucified God will place a demand on our lives. It
will be all or nothing—either the totality of our lives or the nothing of
the self-centered ego. One cannot really pray in union with a crucified
God without ultimately becoming crucified in one's own life. This path
of prayer is to awaken our minds and hearts to the truth that the body
of Christ does not exist without us. The way to peace requires the fullness of Christ and the meaning of Christian life is to live the Christ
mystery. To become "another Christ" does not mean to become a male
Jew but to become our true selves, to come to the truth of our identity,
and in this true self-knowledge to find the freedom to love. We *are* the
body of Christ, each of us with our own bodies and spirits, minds and
hearts. Each of us is Christ because each of us is created through the
Word and is a little word incarnate, which longs to express itself
through the Spirit of love. "God utters me like a word containing a par-
tial thought of himself," Merton wrote.[33] Christianity is not merely a
doctrine or a system of beliefs. Rather, we are Christian because we
believe that we and all creation find meaning and purpose in Christ. But
until we allow this mystery of Christ to touch us, embrace us and
change us, we remain outside the mystery. Christ remains distant to us,
as if Christ was a movie star, a person different from us in the same way
that our neighbors or our co-workers are different from us. But Christ
is not outside us; rather, Christ lives in us. We are Christ, members of
Christ's body through the Spirit. In his last conference in Bangkok,

Thomas Merton sought to explore the Christ mystery in a global context and spoke on the spirituality of nonviolence: "What we are asked to do at present is not so much to speak of Christ as to let him live in us so that people may find him by feeling how he lives in us."[34]

If we hope for a future of peace, then we must create that future of peace. Crucified love is love for the sake of the other that makes space for the other to enter and share life. It is the love of a new future because it forgives past deeds and stretches forward in hope and in the joy of the Spirit. If we desire a future of peace then we must make that peace real by becoming peace. Christ crucified is the way to peace. How to live this way is the path of Franciscan prayer, from gazing on the mirror of God's love for us to becoming that crucified love in one's own life. This path promises not only a new creation but a new future—new hope, new birth, new life—not only for humankind but for the earth and all the galaxies of the universe because peace is rooted in God.

Francis of Assisi became a new creation in Christ and the world around him became more Christic. He became a peacemaker and proclaimed peace by his example and deeds, bringing peace to those in conflict and saying to those he met along the way: "May the Lord give your peace!" Clare of Assisi saw Francis as an example and mirror of Christ and mapped out the way to be an active member of Christ's body, bearing the message of peace and salvation by our lives. Bonaventure sought peace and found it in the burning love of the crucified Christ, a path he claimed which could only be traveled by the poor and humble. The path to peace is the path of ecstatic love by which one is not afraid to die with Christ crucified and rise to new life in the dominance of grace. In his search for peace, Bonaventure concluded with these words:

> Whoever loves this death can see God because it is true beyond doubt that man will not see me and live. Let us, then, die and enter into the darkness; let us impose silence upon our cares, our desires and our imaginings. With Christ crucified let us pass out of this world to the Father so that when the Father is shown to us, we may say with Philip: It is

enough for us. Let us hear with Paul: *My grace is sufficient for you.* Let us rejoice with David saying: *My flesh and my heart have grown faint; You are the God of my heart, and the God that is my portion forever.*"[36]

If we hope for peace then we must desire love, the love that is of God and centered in God. The Franciscan path of prayer is a path of conversion, a disarmament of the heart so that we can attain that love by which we become God's instruments for the disarmament of the world. It is a path that takes seriously the woundedness of humanity and creation because it is here in the fragility of life that God dwells in humble love. It is a path that ultimately proclaims, "brothers and sisters, we are one," because on this path we come to see God's goodness as the luminous web that binds together all of humanity and creation. But we also see—if we see truthfully—what we are not. We see that we are fragmented, divisive, dominating and oppressive. And so we must travel the path through the burning love of the crucified Christ. One who descends into the depth of the Christ mystery ascends to the height of transcendent love, a love which is not self-centered but that goes out of itself for the sake of the other. We are called to be that eucharistic embrace of forgiveness and reconciliation in a broken world. This is the path of prayer that leads to peace. It is the path of Franciscan evangelical life. It is the path of Christian life. If we hope for peace, it is what is ours to do.

Meditation

Take some time to reflect on peace in your life. Consider whether or not peace is at the center of your life or what prevents you from enjoying peace. Reflect on the Christian vocation of peacemaking and try to see the connection between peace in your heart and peace in the world. The following words of Bonaventure may help your meditation:

> Peace cannot be had without charity. As soon as we acquire charity, all that pertains to perfection becomes easy: acting or suffering, living or dying. We must therefore endeavor to advance in love, for perfect love leads to perfection in all else. (*The Triple Way*)

As you continue to meditate on the relationship between love and peace, consider the following questions:

1. Francis traveled the path of peace through the cross of Jesus Christ. Are you willing to travel the same path? What is your understanding of peace?

2. What are the obstacles to peace in your own life? How can prayer help you overcome these obstacles?

3. Do you view the Eucharist as personal devotion or public witness? How can prayer help you to become a "eucharistic person"?

4. What are some ways you can relate the Eucharist to your concern for peace and justice?

NOTES

[1] This is Bonaventure's idea of perfect love as he describes it in his spiritual work, *The Triple Way*. See Bonaventure, *Triplicia via* 2.11 (VIII, 10). Engl. trans. de Vinck, "The Triple Way or Love Enkindled," 78. In his *Breviloquium* Bonaventure explains the order of charity as love of God, love of our self, love of neighbor equally as our self and love of body. See *Breviloquium* 5.8 (V, 261).

[2] Walter Wink, *Engaging the Powers* (Minneapolis: Fortress Press, 1992), 217.

[3] The Anonymous of Perugia," 8.38. Engl. trans. *FA:ED* II, 52–53.

[4] Thomas of Celano. "Life of Saint Francis," 10. Engl. trans. *FA:ED* I, 203.

[5] Thomas of Celano, "Life of Saint Francis," 12. Engl. trans. *FA:ED* I, 207.

[6] John Dear, *The God of Peace: Toward a Theology of Nonviolence* (Maryknoll, NY: Orbis, 1994), 167.

[7] Daniel Berrigan, *To Dwell in Peace* (San Francisco: Harper & Row, 1987), 163–64.

[8] Bonaventure, *Leg. maj.* 8.6 (EM, 68). Engl. trans. *FA:ED* II, 590.

[9] According to the *Oxford Latin Dictionary*, the word *pietas* is defined as "an attitude of respect toward those to whom one is bound by ties of religion, consanguinity; of relationships between human beings: a. of children to parents, b. of parents to children, c. between husband and wife, d. of other relationships." See *Oxford Latin Dictionary*, ed. P. G.W. Glare (Oxford: Clarendon Press, 1982, repr. 1983), 1378.

[10] Bonaventure, *Leg. maj.* 8.1 (EM, 64). Engl. trans. *FA:ED* II, 586.

[11] Thomas of Celano, "Remembrance of the Desire of a Soul" 124. Engl. trans. *FA:ED* II, 354.

[12] Thomas of Celano, "First Life of Saint Francis" 250–51. Engl. trans. *FA:ED* I, 250–51.

[13] Timothy Vining, "A Theology of Creation Based on the Life of Francis of Assisi," *Cord* 40 (1990): 105.

[14] Bonaventure, *Leg. maj* 8.6 (EM, 68). Engl. trans. *FA:ED* II, 590.

[15] Francis of Assisi, *Admonition* 15 (*Écrits*, 106). Engl. trans. *FA:ED* I, 134.

[16] Francis of Assisi, "The Canticle of the Creatures" 10–11 (*Écrits*, 344). Engl. trans. *FA:ED* I, 114.

[17] Holmes Rolston III, "Kenosis and Nature," in *The Works of Love*, 59.

[18] Bonaventure, *Hex.* 22.23 (V, 441).

[19] Francis of Assisi, "A Letter to the Entire Order" 12–13 (*Écrits*, 246). Engl. trans. *FA:ED* I, 117.

[20] Volf, *Exclusion and Embrace*, 48.

[21] Ibid., 51.

[22] Ibid., 129.

[23] Ibid., 128.

[24] Ibid.

[25] Ibid., 131.

[26] Bruteau, *Grand Option*, 171.

[27] See Ilia Delio, "Francis and the Body of Christ," *Cord* 53.1 (2003): 26–35.

[28] Merton, *New Seeds of Contemplation*, 75.

[29] Merton, *New Seeds of Contemplation*, 71.

[30] Oscar Romero, *The Violence of Love*, ed. James Brockman (San Francisco: Harper & Row, 1988), 43. In his struggle to emphasize the peacemaking mission of the church Romero proclaimed: "An accommodating church, a church that seeks prestige without the pain of the cross is not the authentic church of Jesus Christ."

[31] James Washington, *A Testament of Hope: The Essential Writings of Martin Luther King, Jr.* (San Francisco: Harper & Row, 1986), 298–300.

[32] Merton, *New Seeds of Contemplation*, 37.

[33] Thomas Merton, quoted in James Forest, *Living With Wisdom: A Life of Thomas Merton* (Maryknoll, NY: Orbis Books, 1991), 216.

[34] Itin. 7.6 (V, 312). Engl. trans. Cousins, *Bonaventure*, 116.

CONCLUSION

With so many prayer methods abounding today people often ask, which method is right for me? It is an important question because not every "method" of prayer is suitable to Christian life. Gnostic prayer, new age prayer, dualistic prayer and other prayer "types" may lead some on paths they may have preferred not to go.

What I have tried to do in this book is to lay out a path of prayer that is distinctly Franciscan and Christian for, indeed, Franciscan spirituality is fundamentally Christian. In this respect, to understand the path of Franciscan prayer is not simply to learn a new "type" of prayer but to understand how prayer shapes a person for gospel living—"living" because Christian life is a daily struggle and challenge to follow Christ.

The simplest way to describe Franciscan prayer is that it begins and ends with the Incarnation. It begins with encountering the God of overflowing love in the person of Jesus Christ and ends with embodying that love in one's own life, becoming a new Incarnation. This is what it means to live the gospel life—not simply doing what Jesus did but opening up oneself to God who descends and takes on human flesh anew in the life of the believer. To live the gospel life is to proclaim by one's life the Good News of God among us and thus to make Jesus Christ live anew. While the path of Franciscan prayer leads to a renewal of Incarnation, becoming a new body of Christ, this does not mean, of course, that there are many different Christs. Rather, there is one Christ, the fullness of which is marked by a diversity of members (as Bonaventure wrote in his *Breviloquium*), indeed, by the diversity of creation itself. In the western Christian tradition, we tend to think of Christ only in terms of Jesus of Nazareth. But the Franciscans conceived of the Christ mystery much more broadly. Incarnation is what all of creation is about because it is the Word of God made flesh. We who claim to be Christian are caught up in the mystery of Christ in an explicit way. To be caught up in this mystery is to be caught up in a God of "reckless love"—reckless enough to remain faithful in love in suffering and death. We are called to find this God in fragile human flesh, encounter him and let ourselves be fully embraced by him. To encounter this God of humble love, however, does not demand that we first look inside ourselves in some type of "detached" introspection. On the contrary we are asked to look long and hard at the person of Jesus Christ, especially in the concrete details of the cross. It is here that we can begin to know God and ourselves in God. Gazing in this way will ultimately lead us to our true identity in God.

Although we must first encounter God *without* to find God *within*, once we find God within we are eager to look more deeply without. Meeting God in the crucified Christ is reason to search the depths of our lives, the image of God in which we are created. However, the God within us is the God who permeates every aspect of our world—the one who is the source and goal of creation. Thus, once we enter on this path of prayer and become more related to God in and through the mystery of Christ, the more we begin to look closely at the world around us— our neighbors, spouses, brothers, sisters, stars, moon, trees, rivers. And the more closely we look, the more we see things in a new way. As we enter more deeply into the Christ mystery in our own lives, we come to see that each created being shares in this mystery. Not only is creation sacramental in a general sense, but each star, cricket, proton, leper, poor person reflects the overflowing goodness of God precisely in the distinction of its features and the very uniqueness in which each person or thing is created. Each person and creature of creation is singularly loved into being by God. The prayerful person who is deeply in love with God realizes that the whole universe is the cloister to find God. That is, one does not have to leave the world to find God. Rather, one finds God expressed in the details of the world. It is Christ who is the guide to the cloister of the universe. One who enters into the mystery of Christ and who lives in Christ knows Christ as the center of the universe, because Christ is the Word made flesh, the Word of God through whom all things are made, the Word who took on our frail human nature and is now risen and glorified.

The path of Franciscan prayer is deep and profound. One cannot skip through it by saying a few quick prayers before the cross. Rather, the one who prays must be like a seeker of fine pearls who searches the depths of the Christ mystery in creation. Prayer in this tradition requires long hours of solitude, time alone to gaze and be with the God of overflowing love. When we search long and hard enough to know the source of our own lives and the source of life at the heart of creation, we discover that the whole creation is pregnant with God. To see, to contemplate and to be transformed so as to become what we love marks the path of Franciscan prayer.

The problem today is that we love many things—our freedom, independence, financial wealth, status, power and whatever else our culture tells us will make us happy; thus, there is little room within us to fully embrace God. God, in a sense, has to push through all the things that clutter our lives in order to dwell within us. Franciscan prayer calls us back to poverty, penance, conversion and a heart full of mercy, values and attitudes that are counter-cultural but life-giving. Only when we acknowledge our need for God can we begin to find God. Prayer begins in the poverty of the desert and is the cry of the poor person who is far from home and seeks the way to the source of life.

The mark of our relationship with God is freedom. Franciscan prayer reminds us that God loves us freely and calls us to love freely. We are not forced to become the body of Christ, we are invited by God's grace into the banquet of life. It is precisely for this reason that Christian life is obscure today in western culture. We have so many other invitations to consider, it is difficult to discern the invitation of a humble God bent over in love. Our tendency, therefore, is to participate in the rituals of prayer and worship with little extra effort. We do what is perfunctory and then we expect God to do the rest. The Franciscan path of prayer, centered on the Incarnation, tells us that God is with us, but will not bring about the fullness of life without us. *Our complete participation is required.* We are not simply to pray—we are to become prayer—living flames of love that ignite the world. Fire is a constant image in the writings of Bonaventure primarily because it represented for him the intensity of love. Love is attractive, and living in the intensity of love is alluring, but when we come to understand the demands of love we withdraw our resolution to pray. We fear the demands of love and prefer mediocre lives that remain unfulfilled. We prefer the safety and comfort of individualism and isolationism than the risk of relationship. For love, like prayer, is relational. Only when we attain a deep relationship with God can we dare to love in a way that is transforming. Prayer is to lead us into the depths of transforming love, so that the image in which we are created can shine out as the presence of God among us, and we can proclaim the Good News of Jesus Christ: "This is my body, this is my blood"—not with words but with the example of our lives.

At the heart of it all, Franciscan prayer is about gospel living. It is not really concerned with knowledge or intellectual contemplation. It is concerned with the human person and the transformation of the human person in God. It is about living Christ and making the Good News of the Incarnation alive. How desperately this path of prayer is needed in our world today! We seek healing of divisions, hate and violence. We desire wholeness, unity and peace. How shall these things come about? Are they merely ideas or values that must be given flesh and blood? To live the gospel is to put flesh and blood on God and proclaim throughout the universe, the glory of God is fully alive! Without flesh and blood, the Good News that God has become human and healed the divisions of humankind and all creation is not news at all. Christian life demands human participation or it simply does not exist. It is an empty title in a broken world. If we desire justice, peace and love among humankind and throughout creation, then we humans must become justice, peace and love. This is the Good News of Jesus Christ and the Good News of being Christian—to live in the depths of God's faithful love in a way that resounds throughout all creation. The path of Franciscan prayer is a way to live fully the Gospel life by living fully in the mystery of Christ. We must descend with Christ into the darkness of our humanity so that we may rise with Christ in the unity of love. In a world marked by violence and death, suffering does not have the last word. The last word is love and that love is the fullness of Christ, the Word of God.

> O God,
> I pray that I may know You and love You
> So as eternally to rejoice in You.
> And if, in the present life, I cannot do so fully,
> Grant that my love and knowledge may at least grow on earth
> That my joy may be fully in heaven:
> A joy expected here and there fulfilled.
> O Lord our Father,
> You counseled, or rather commanded through Your Son,
> That we ask for this fullness of joy; and You promised to grant it.
> I ask of You, O Lord, that which, through Your Wonder-Counselor,
> You encouraged us to ask and promised to grant:
> That our joy may be full!
> Let my mind meditate on this joy, my tongue speak of it,
> My heart desire it, my words extol it,
> My soul hunger for it, my flesh thirst for it,
> My whole substance yearn for it,
> Until I enter into the joy of my God
> Who is Triune and One,
> Blessed forever.
> Amen.
>
> —Bonaventure
> Soliloquy

SELECT BIBLIOGRAPHY

BOOKS

Armstrong, Regis J. *St. Francis of Assisi*. New York: Crossroad, 1994.

Angela of Foligno: Complete Works. Translated by Paul Lachance. Mahwah: Paulist, 1993.

Balthasar, Hans Urs von. *Studies in Theological Style: Clerical Styles*. Translatedby Andrew Louth, Francis McDonagh and Brian McNeil. Vol. 2. *The Glory of the Lord. A Theological Aesthetics*. Edited by Joseph Fessio. San Francisco: Ignatius, 1984.

Bringing Forth Christ, the Son of God. Five Feasts of the Child Jesus. St. Bonaventure. Translated by Eric Doyle. Oxford: SLG Press, 1984.

Bonaventure. *The Soul's Journey into God, The Tree of Life, The Life of St. Francis*. Translation and introduction by Ewert Cousins. New York: Paulist, 1978.

Bruteau, Beatrice. *The Grand Option: Personal Transformation and a New Creation*. Notre Dame, Ind.: University of Notre Dame, 2001.

Clare of Assisi: Early Documents. Translation and introduction by Regis J. Armstrong. New York: The Franciscan Institute, 1993.

Cousins, Ewert. *Bonaventure and the Coincidence of Opposites*. Chicago: Franciscan Herald Press, 1978.

Dear, John. *The God of Peace: Toward a Theology of Nonviolence*. Maryknoll, N.Y.: Orbis, 1994.

Doyle, Eric. *St. Francis and the Song of Brotherhood*. New York: Seabury Press, 1981.

Delio, Ilia. *Crucified Love: Bonaventure's Mysticism of the Crucified Christ*. Quincy, Ill.: Franciscan Press, 1998.

——. *Simply Bonaventure: An Introduction to his Life, Thought, and Writings*. New York: New City Press, 2001.

Francis of Assisi: Early Documents. Volume 1. *The Saint*. Edited by Regis J. Armstrong, J. A. Wayne Hellmann, and William J. Short. New York: New City Press, 1999.

Francis of Assisi: Early Documents. Volume 2. *The Founder*. Edited by Regis J. Armstrong, J. A. Wayne Hellmann, and William J. Short. New York: New City Press, 2000.

Hayes, Zachary. *The Hidden Center: Spirituality and Speculative Christology in St. Bonaventure*. New York: The Franciscan Institute, 1992.

Johnson, Timothy J. *The Soul in Ascent: Bonaventure on Poverty, Prayer and Union* with God. New York: New City Press, 2000.

————(ed.). *Bonaventure. Mystic of God's Word: Selected Spiritual Writings*. Quincy, Ill.: Franciscan Press, 2000.

Lull, Ramón. *The Book of the Lover and the Beloved*. Edited by Kenneth Leech from the E. Allison Peers translation of Ramón Lull. Paulist Press, 1978.

Marion, Jean-Luc. *God Without Being*. Translated by Thomas A. Carlson. Chicago: University of Chicago Press, 1991.

Merton, Thomas. *New Seeds of Contemplation*. New York: New Directions Books,1961.

Moltmann, Jürgen. *The Crucified God: The Cross of Christ as the Foundation and Criticism of Christian Theology*. Translated by R.A. Wilson and John Bowden. San Francisco: Harper, 1991.

————. *God in Creation: A Theology of Creation and the Spirit of God*. Translated by Margaret Kohl. Minneapolis: Fortress, 1993.

Polkinghorne, John (ed.). *The Work of Love: Creation as Kenosis*. Grand Rapids, Mich.: Wm. B. Eerdmans, 2001.

The Works of St. Bonaventure. 5 Volumes. Translated by José de Vinck. Paterson, N.J.: St. Anthony Guild Press, 1960–1970.

Volf, Miroslav. *Exclusion and Embrace: A Theological Exploration of Identity, Otherness, and Reconciliation*. Nashville: Abingdon Press, 1996.

What Manner of Man? Sermons on Christ by St. Bonaventure. Introduction and translation by Zachary Hayes. 2nd edition. Chicago: Franciscan Herald Press, 1989.

Ulanov, Barry and Ann. *Primary Speech. A Psychology of Prayer*. Atlanta: John Knox Press, 1982.

ARTICLES

Beha, Maria. "Praying with Clare of Assisi." *Cord* 47.4 (1997): 185–93.

Blastic, Michael W. "Contemplation and Compassion: A Franciscan Ministerial Spirituality." In *Spirit and Life: A Journal of Contemporary Franciscanism*. Edited by Anthony Carrozzo, Kenneth Himes and Vincent Cushing. New York: The Franciscan Institute, 1997.

Brunelli, Delir, " 'Contemplation in the Following of Jesus Christ' The Experience of Clare of Assisi." *Cord* 52.4 (2002): 154–70.

Grygus, John. "Poverty and Prayer: The Franciscan Way to God." *Cord* 39 (1989): 35–50.

Hellmann, J.A. Wayne. "Poverty: The Franciscan Way to God." *Theology Digest* 22 (1975): 239–45.

Hubaut, Michael. "Christ, Our Joy." Translated by Paul Barrett. *Greyfriars Review* 9 (1995, Supplement).

SELECT BIBLIOGRAPHY

Johnson, Timothy J. "Speak Lord, Your Servant is Listening: Prayer and Obedience in St. Francis." *Cord* 42 (1992): 36–45.

Lamoureux, Richard E. "Prayer as Desire: An American View." *Review for Religious* (1990): 664–73.

Laurance, John D. "The Eucharist as the Imitation of Christ." *Theological Studies* 47 (1986): 286–96.

Lehmann, Leonhard. "St. Francis at Prayer—Introduction." *Greyfriars Review* 10.3 (1996): 223–34.

———. "Francis' Marian Prayers." *Greyfriars Review* 13 (1999): 1–20.

MacGinty, Gerald. "Lectio Divina: Font and Guide of the Spiritual Life." *Cistercian Studies* 21.1 (1986): 64–71.

Matura, Thaddée. "The Heart Turned Towards the Lord." *Cord* 44 (1994): 4–15.

Mullholland, Seamus. "The Form of St. Francis' Prayer: Models for Creative Diversity Today." *Cord* 41 (1991): 296–306.

Purfield, Brian. "Francis of Assisi and Unceasing Prayer." *Cord* 39 (1989): 19–31.

Raguin, Yves. "Poverty and Prayer." *Contemplative Review* 19 (1986): 28–36. Sandor, Monica. "Lectio Divina and the Monastic Spirituality of Reading." *American Benedictine Review* 40 (1989): 82–114.

Schmucki, Octavian. "Place of Solitude: An Essay on the External Circumstances of the Prayer Life of St. Francis of Assisi." Translated by Sebastian Holland. *Greyfriars Review* 2 (1988): 77–132.

Van Asseldonk, Optatus. "The Spirit of the Lord and Its Holy Activity in the Writings of Francis." *Greyfriars Review* 5 (1991): 104–58.

Van den Goorbergh, Edith. "Clare's Prayer as a Spiritual Journey." *Greyfriars Review* 10 (1996): 283–92.

INDEX